CW00541404

To Elise Keep Kickin

Dean

Williams

Dahollow

MARTIAL MASTERS Vol 1

MARTIAL

MASTERS

Volume 1

Dan Holloway

& Lucci Del-Gaudio

First published in 2016 in the UK

3P Publishing Ltd
C E C, London Road
Corby
NN17 5EU

A catalogue number for this book is available from

the British Library

ISBN 978-1-911559-06-1

For my family that have always supported me in my martial arts training, along with all my different instructors over the years.

Dan Holloway

For Anthony Pillage, his speech at the MAI Awards in 2014 inspired this book and for the help he gave me promoting seminars that helped to elevate my name on the circuit. And my dog.

Lucci Del-Gaudio

Foreword

Lucci and I first came up with the idea for *Martial Masters* in October 2015 after meeting and training with a lot of people in the martial arts circuit through our work with Martial Artists Supporting Children with Cancer. We were meeting incredible martial artists, all from different backgrounds who were coming together to showcase their styles, all for the fantastic cause of raising money for children with cancer. There was no ego, no bickering about what style is best or what would work in a fight; just genuine people showing their support for what Lucci had set up. This, to us, was what martial arts should be about.

Anyone reading this book probably has an interest to some degree in martial arts, and it's fair to say that martial artists are infamous for bickering and fighting amongst themselves about different styles or what will and won't work. With this book we aimed to bring people from all disciplines together, genuine people who are putting themselves out there and doing good work for the martial arts industry as a whole. People from traditional backgrounds, to sport and self defence are in this book and this is what sets us apart. Look at any martial arts section on Amazon, or in Waterstones, and you'll find books dedicated to Judo, Aikido, Kung Fu or Reality Based Self Defence. Interviews are done with leading figures in the field, yet no book out there has bought these styles together in a collaborative fashion as we have.

With Volume 1 of this book, we have focused on UK martial arts, and have been lucky enough to interview some true legends in the martial arts industry. From Guro Bob Breen who is known as the Godfather of JKD in Europe, to Andy Norman who is paving the way in professionalising the martial arts industry, we have individuals who are putting their system out there and trying to make a change. We wanted to hear about their journey, what inspires them and how they got to the place they are now and what will happen in the future.

It is our intention with this book to open the martial arts industry's eyes and show that collaboration and working together is beneficial to the martial arts industry as a whole. The same people who claim to promote honesty, integrity and respect are often the first ones bad mouthing other styles or having petty arguments with other instructors. The individuals in this book do their thing and follow their own path, helping the community around them and building strong martial artists who will pass on their teachings in the future.

This is only Volume 1 of Martial Masters and there are plans for many more to follow including international volumes! We hope you enjoy this book, read about some of the main players in the martial arts field and maybe even be a little bit inspired by what they have achieved.

Thanks to everyone who has supported us in this venture, it has been a steep learning curve for us both, but here it is – Martial Masters Volume 1. Enjoy!

Dan Holloway

Contents

MARTIAL MASTERS

Volume One

The interviews

Scott Caldwell

REAL Fighting System

Scott is the man behind REAL Fighting system. With a background in everything from Boxing to Krav Maga, he has led an interesting life and has an understanding and experience of violence that many of us would hope never to gain. All his real world experience has led him to create REAL Fighting which he now teaches through seminars and his own training facility.

One of the highly successful Martial Arts Guardians, Scott promotes a no-nonsense approach to violence drawing on his real experience as well as martial arts training. Anyone who knows Scott will know he's slightly mental so it was both a pleasure and an eye opener to interview the man behind REAL Fighting.

You have a pretty interesting background in Martial Arts Scott, can you tell us where it all began for you?

I have a background in everything from Judo, Karate, Kickboxing, Boxing, Urban Krav Maga so I guess so! I think it depends on how long you spend with someone and what you take out of it. For me, I know students in martial arts that have done 30-40 years and have never grasped the real concept of what it is they are doing. I know other people that pick something up in 2 minutes and can break it down and tell you whether it's real or not!

I started with Judo at 7. I was far too energetic and was always getting into trouble and my mother didn't really have a great idea of what to do with me and all that energy. My uncle got a grip of me and said "come on then I'll take you to the local judo club", which at the time was held in a Red Cross Hall. It was a completely concreted floor with nothing more than a canvas spread that we put down so if you fell…you fell! You had to learn to fall pretty quickly!!

How long did you do Judo for, was it something you really got in to?

Yeah, it was great. I did it up to green belt which is the 5th or 6th belt but with tags in between as well so it would have taken you about 1000 years to become a black belt in Judo in the old days! I used to get thrown around all over the place and absolutely loved it! What I didn't like about the Judo was the fact I'd fight with someone but naturally want to put my hands on them once they got me into a position and obviously there's no punching or kicking. I not only found that pretty limiting, but also quite strange in a way, you're learning to fight, but within the fight you can't do certain things. I kind of blew it off for a while and started boxing, but found the same thing really, I wanted to get a grip of someone and get in a better position to hit them, and obviously that isn't allowed. I found limitations very, very early on within my training and found it very frustrating.

So what did you find after that, you tried Boxing and Judo and found the limitations, what was next? Did you consciously think, I want a stand up game, I want a wrestling game and a ground game and search for it?

I just wanted to be able to fight without restriction and so bounced between the two for a little while then left for a little while and went back to fighting on the streets which was always a constant. I then got into Shotokan Karate at around 11 or 12 years old. I did that for a few years, again on and off. My background in martial arts has been for 35 years but very sporadic in the early days where my lack of discipline got the better of me and my frustrations got the better of me so I left and came back repeatedly. I was a wild kid and if something wasn't sitting right with me I wouldn't stay.

Do you think the martial arts helped to tone that down at all or were you just not finding the right thing?

Martial arts did a hell of a lot more for me than I realised at the time. It was more obvious when I wasn't doing martial arts how much it was helping me when I was. I was getting into street fights from a very early age, my accent and attitude attracted a lot of attention. There were always the street fights and I knocked about with kids a lot older than me and would literally walk head first into a burning building with the older kids who were entertained by how I was. I was put in to a lot of very precarious positions due to the fact I was knocking about with older kids and there was quite a bit of bullying and peer pressure. I went through a couple of very

very dark years of being bullied in an environment that I had chosen for myself that I kind of refused to walk away from. I suffered quite badly for a couple of years from around the age of 6 and 8.

A lot of people shy away from this subject, but I've spoken to students and people I train and it's an important aspect of what I teach, but I was also going through a habitual sexual nightmare. So between the bullying and that nightmare I was pretty close to the edge. I talk about this quite openly and honestly with my students, but I was getting close to the edge and feeling like I was losing myself. The abuse I was suffering nearly got me for the final time and I was pinned against the wall and just stopped fighting back and was just letting it happen. When you're 8 years of age, I don't think you can have a conscious, emotionally intelligent thought that if you don't fight back now that could be the end for you but that's what I felt. Instantly, I fought back though and I've never looked back since or let myself become the victim again, I've obliterated everything in front of me. Nobody will ever put me in a position where I'm that close to losing me again.

Were you still training martial arts at this point, when did you find the Krav Maga?

It was in and out mate, I might train for a month then they wouldn't see me for a month. I used to privately train with an ex-squaddy called John Anderson, but I was in London, had done a bit of Kickboxing and Boxing a bit to keep my hand in, but I was moving round a little bit. I had been on the run in Dublin, Liverpool and a few different places so I always trained in whatever people were training in, it didn't matter to me. I just wanted to keep fit and keep my hand in. This guy John Anderson had done quite a bit of Krav, I'm not sure what his qualifications were, but I loved the directness of it, the venom of it. But even within that, the more familiar I became with it, the more restriction I found. For me whatever works, end of story. The more familiar I got with Krav Maga, the more I found the politics and restrictions, if it wins a fight, who gives a fuck? I began to just train my own way and I'm well publicised for the kinds of things I did for a living so I was at the sharp end a lot.

You're known for being somewhat of a maverick in the martial arts and self defence world and have led a pretty interesting life! Can you give us some of the juice and dirt on your escapades? Don't spare the gory details.

Jesus, I was a professional bastard, not always for the wrong side but often, for the best part of twenty years, so it's a large question, my friend.

A bastard in what way? What was your job at the time?

Job titles are for Tesco employees, bank workers and ordinary everyday people, I never wore a name tag identifying what I was so it's a difficult question to answer but the short version is whatever it took.

There are enough people out there who don't mind taking on the role of Hans Christian Anderson with tales of my life and never let the truth get in the way so if you want sensationalism you should speak to them but I like my freedom. Those who know me will tell you I never tell old 'war stories' apart from the same couple that appeal to my dark sense of humour or serve as a lesson to others. I will say that, I've been a persuader of those who needed convincing, a collector from those who didn't believe in paying their debts, a protector to those who had something to lose, chaired meetings while providing security or insurance for disputing parties and been someone who could be called upon at a moment's notice. I spent time in UK and European cities making alliances or removing obstacles for those that needed it to further their ends and lent my name or presence in order to make the dealings of those who had my number easier. Some of that makes me sound quite honourable but I assure you I was not and most of those I provided a service for you will never see mentioned in the New Year's honours list for charitable acts!

I'm neither proud nor ashamed of my past deeds but at some point that life will come to an abrupt end and much of the time at great personal cost. I have the physical and mental scars to testify to that fact and today I show them honestly in the hope it lends to my teaching. It's no coincidence that while serving 5 years of a 9 year sentence I made the decision to educate ordinary people on how to deal with men like me upon my release. I recognised it was time to give something back and offer my mind some semblance of peace and balance.

While in there I put a lot of time into self-improvement and discovery, worked hard every day in the gym and studied law, psychology and philosophy. I pushed hard to answer questions of myself I would never dared ask previously. The main question being: what in me had driven me and delivered me unceremoniously to my 8x12ft box? The answer? I was in essence a masochist. The violence, abuse and bullying I'd suffered and overcome as a child had left a hole. I believe beyond doubt that we are a product of our experiences and if you force a child to bark long enough he will either become a spaniel of a wolf. Coming through my nightmares had given me a God complex and had made me arrogant, reckless and in need of new dangers to replace the pain and constantly retest myself. The pressures of criminality fitted me like a glove. In other words, I wasn't someone you'd be pleasantly surprised to see sat at your breakfast table quietly tucking into your Sugar Puffs uninvited.

How did those experiences shape your view and perception of violence?

For all my experience I have never become numb to violence or the fear violence promotes within the human conditional, as others claim. That being said, it never kept me hidden under the bed at home or applying for a position as a postie either though. I've come to believe that violence is an ever present possibility in life and it is better to accept that fact and become better at it whether you wish to use it or not. Do I wish it wasn't necessary? I've never allowed myself the time to consider it any more than I would allow myself to cross a busy road with my eyes closed wishing cars didn't exist. Violence, just like cars, are a reality so the green cross code should be learnt.

What's the most violent encounter you've seen/been part of?

Again, I like my freedom so I'll answer this question based on what has been inflicted on me. I think portraying the realities of being on the wrong side of violence is more relevant to what should be taught instead of the usual, 'I killed ten men with my bare hands' bollocks anyway. I've been shot at on a couple of occasions which is a pretty surreal experience, only because it's 'TV violence' and I've had all manner of objects used against my person, which is very visually obvious during the summer months as I have huge stripes of white that won't tan on my head and body. If I had a pound for every time someone has asked how many stitches I have but the answer is less than 30 because I'm a big fan of Gaffer Tape and Superglue.

However, the one encounter that springs to mind more than any other, due to how helpless I was, is having a 3ft broken railing spike brought to the pupil of my eye and being teased with it for what felt like an eternity before it being driven down into my foot while I was held in position. I remember looking at this thing and thinking, 'look at the rust on it for fuck sake', while it was being toyed with in front of me. I recall very little of the verbal exchange. Anyone who has ever been that helpless will testify that your mind dances between reality and beyond and my memory of it has become almost comedic. I do remember as it was finally driven through me a wave of euphoria and almost biblical release of tension leave me and I felt no pain. Shock maybe but to me it was a sense of power and my psychology convinced me I'd controlled its eventual destination, not them. That encounter only served to further feed the masochist in me and convince me of other things I believed of myself. It was a very self destructive path testing those theories.

How did you get out of that path and on to the one you're on now?

In short, my power came from the fact that regardless of the accusations I've had levelled against me there was nothing to support them. A guilty verdict and large prison term kind of changes that so rather than continue I chose to get out. As I said, prison gave me a lot of time to re-evaluate and I wasted little time doing so.

How do you feel about the current state of martial arts and self defence? Do you differentiate between the two? Is the current situation good?

It's an interesting question. I don't differentiate between martial arts and self defence, do other people, perhaps? Martial arts, to me, means exactly that - martial means war. Self defence is protection; it's fighting, and it's war. What's the difference? There shouldn't be one. Different styles may have a different mindset or approach to fighting, but the end game should always be the same and that should be to go home with as little damage as possible while inflicting the most. For me, is there a difference today? Yes, very much so, do I like the differentiation? No! I think some martial arts are so fucking deluded and diluted by salesmen and charlatans that now there is a difference as people see them differently. For me they're exactly the same thing, they were both born out of a need for protection and need to look after yourself.

Do you think the charlatans and salesmen you refer to are more prevalent now than in the past?

I speak to a lot of the old heads who I have the upmost respect for. A lot of the guys who have been in the competition circuit, or just train for the sake of training or for a job. A lot of guys who have been around for a long long time. As long as I have been around martial arts I kept myself very distant from what so and so believes it should be. Therefore, it's not for me to say from an uneducated point of view, but they say "Jesus Christ". There is a very well-known and well respected personality in the martial arts who said that things have gone down and down since the birth of the McDojo and now it's all about the grading and sales and a certificate that really means fuck all as what you've learnt is monkey see monkey do. So, yes to answer your question I've trained with some very talented martial artists, but also some very hard men who wouldn't be considered to be the artistic side of martial arts. I have equal respect for both sides but for different reasons but for me martial is martial.

Do you think there's a place now for business in the martial arts?

It's another great question Dan and it's like a politician. Does he do it for the money, or the love of the people? We all slag politicians off but regardless of the fact they get paid money, they may have gone in to it for the love of the people. There are others that start naively for the love of the people and then greed gets the best of them and their personality. I think it comes down to the personality teaching the martial arts to be honest. I can't broadstroke because I know there are a number of very, very self-conscious and giving people within the martial arts who charge money. However, I also know a number of absolute evil, robbing fuckers who don't care what they teach and just charge their students regardless of effectiveness or background. It's bollocks.

It comes down to the personality, not the art or the time; there were charlatans 50 years ago. I've been told entertaining stories down the years about Japanese 1st Dan's stepping on a plane from Osaka landing here as 6th Dan's and charging extortionate amounts of money to those who simply weren't Japanese. It's just more prevalent now in terms of more sales and the internet.

Let's move on to the Martial Arts Guardians then. Where did the idea come about and how did it develop?

It came about due to myself and Russ Jarmesty talking for quite a long time and having a bit of a joke about the current state of martial arts in some cases. We laugh and joke, but that doesn't mean we don't care, we probably care too much. We were at a famous awards dinner a few years back and looked at each other and just thought we can't do this anymore and allow it to happen. It was kind of an off the cuff conversation which grew. We didn't like being put in the situation we were in and we both knew we both had a pretty loyal following and so thought let's see how far down the rabbit hole they're prepared to follow us. We're going to attack what we feel is wrong. A lot of people were coming to us in private messages or conversation and saying can you do something about the state of what is going on, you guys have a voice, use it. So that's pretty much how it started, we wanted to see how loud the voice was and how far we could push the envelope. I use that analogy as for myself and Russ, that envelope was stuffed with money lining people's pockets through lies and bullshit basically. Russ very, very cleverly brought on Steve Rowe who is probably one of the most decorated martial artists out there and that was a big move. Myself and Russ were seen as the wild kids, the reality guys but Steve Rowe was again, a man of passion. Like us, he's seen it all, but a man who would also protect the traditional side which me and Russ were pretty much trying to smash up at the time as we felt a lot of it was a joke. We wanted to fairly balance things out and that's how Steve came on board. My wife is the designer of the magazine and gives it that incredible feel it has and last, but not least, Simon who has huge experience in the media to basically oversee our naivety. We were a couple of troublesome teens who were basically acting out so we needed someone to rein us in a little journalistically and he did a fantastic job of that.

You said you wanted to see how big that voice got, and it got pretty loud! Even *The Guardian* newspaper kicked off slightly!

Martial Arts Guardian for us was a movement. It had to stop for a little while for a number of reasons. From my own point of view, we had the legal issue. *The Guardian* put us in and we ended up in around 10 national newspapers with interviews etc, but there were a number of other things going on as well. It was my role to glue everyone together and it was just time to knock it on the head for a little while as I was getting bogged down by those who now saw us as the answer to everything, including internal dojo disputes. That's got fuck all to do with why we did this but my time was swallowed by this type of thing.

Are there plans for a return?

Yes! We have an issue almost finished and ready to re-launch. It will become a quarterly magazine. We unfortunately lost Simon and Steve, but have brought on some fantastic people, including you and Lucci to fill that void and it can only go from strength to strength. But giving it the time it needs is difficult sometimes which is why it has to go quarterly. There is no one else putting out 100 pages a month of pure quality, no sales or bullshit and we're trying to keep that but we'll be running out of people and fuck putting Bruce Lee in every second issue or allowing 100 McDojos to advertise because we've run out of ideas on how to fill the pages. We had to review how often to put it out so decided on quarterly.

Going back to yourself, then are you still instructing and keeping your hand in?

Basically I've got back to my own thing. I've committed to private clients and seminars. I have a loyal following that I teach and a few organisations that I'm supposedly not allowed to talk about too much. The easiest way to answer that question is that I have my private students and I fly in and out in order to do the other stuff. Basically my dojo still exists and my assistant who has been with me for a long, long time runs my day to day classes. I go in and make sure I keep an eye on standards etc. My day to day teaching in regular classes is over, but my learning and other teaching is far from over.

What do you think makes a good martial arts instructor?

For me it's about being as real as you possibly can which is impossible if you teach style. If you teach style you have to teach it a certain way. I know a lot of instructors who don't necessarily believe in some of the stuff they teach, but have to teach it anyway as it's part of the syllabus. Anybody who can honestly and openly explain to their students and individualise with their students, establishing a relationship, makes them a good instructor. Understanding their limitations and using them is key to being a good instructor. If you can identify the strength and weaknesses of individuals then they're on their way to being a good instructor.

Where do you see martial arts going in the future?

There's a lot of change going on within martial arts at the moment. We came out as we weren't going to stand by and watch what we were seeing going on. You have absolute legends like Alfie Lewis saying he's not happy with the state of tournaments and so set up the WMO which seems to have gone from strength to strength over the last few months. People are trying to make a difference.

Martial arts are about conformity, you must punch and kick this way, and conformity is something that has spread like a disease to the point of the community outside of the dojo. Everyone is afraid to say what they think unless it's through a private message or telephone call. The more people who stand up for what they believe in and gain followers the better, but it's difficult. Without wishing to sound all mystical and Harry Potter, you have some very odd forces at work out there who are turning good forces against each other, whispering in corners and infecting. It's therefore very difficult. It's divide and conquer for some but we're trying our best as they are! We'll have to see who wins in the end!

What are your plans then for 2017?

I knew whether my training was good or not as I was testing it on a professional level. Obviously I have a different life now and I'm a family man and I try to live my life in a much cleaner way than previously but my training has suffered and that's why I lost some of the passion as I wasn't testing it to the same degree. I need to be able to have 100% conviction in telling someone what works or doesn't work so I decided I needed to be a little more selfish over the next 3 years until I'm 45 to test myself on different stages. I've started with a bare knuckle boxing promotion so I will put myself on that stage and see how I do. A lot of it is testing myself in my seminars which a few are booked and I'm looking forward to just putting myself out there a little bit more. A lot of people have trained with me on other people's seminars or seen me online, but I don't mind admitting I get solid interest in what I do worldwide. What I do is just simplicity with ferocity, it's not rocket science, and I'm not talented enough for anything else so it's just the most natural route for me and it has gone down really well. My concentration will always be with the Urban Krav Maga, but also my REAL fighting which is just a stripped down version of everything I've every learned and used so it has to be up to scratch!

Tony Bailey

Ju-Jitsu

Tony Bailey started martial arts in 1976 when TVs had just gone colour! He started in Basingstoke doing Judo and still has an affiliation with that club 40 years later. His teacher, Sensei Len, recently came up with him to the British Martial Arts Awards so is still keeping his hand in too. He then diversified into lots of different arts mainly around the Ju-Jitsu areas but also some Wado Ryu and Chinese Kung Fu.

He is a Shodan in the Samurai Koryu art of Tenjin Shinyo Ryu Ju Jutsu, a Reiki Master Practitioner and Teacher and holds Dan grades ranging from 1st to 7th Dan in Judo, Kickboxing, Aikido, Weapons,

Combat Ju Jitsu, Aikijujitsu, Kyusho Jutsu and Gendai Ju Jitsu. He has over 21 years experience as a Doorman and Bodyguard and still trains in Basingstoke, running the Basingstoke Ju-Jitsu club which has been going for 22 years with it's own modern syllabus.

Let's start at the beginning, what got you into the martial arts and why?

It was my dad's idea to get my brothers and I into the martial arts so that we would have a system of self defence to protect us. At the time and in my area, Judo was really prevalent and there were 7 different clubs in a town of around 120,000 people which were all rammed! There were waiting lists for every single club and there were many other clubs for different martial arts as well.

We got into the Judo as my dad's background was in Greco-Roman Wrestling and he used to train with all the top Olympic guys in London when he was living there. He wasn't part of the Olympic squad but everyone he trained with was, so he had pretty cool people to train with. He'd been in a few scuffles and been stabbed as a young adult when helping a lady out who was being mugged, He never caused trouble as he was a quiet guy, but he stood up for what was right and knew the importance of grappling in a street fight. As a result of that he wanted to get us into something that would be useful and so we went to the local judo club and started there. We had a trial lesson and I just got on with it really well, good instructors, good atmosphere and everyone there was just really into it, no attitudes or egos. I never really looked back from then. They allowed me to start 6 months earlier than I should have done as there was an age limit, but because of my interest and the fact my dad had come from a great background they said "sure come along and start now".

Judo has always been a constant in my life. Even when I diversified into different arts I was still training at the same judo club and was around 14 when I started helping out teaching, becoming one of the assistant instructors. All the time when I was doing other stuff I'd still go to the club and I still have some friends today from back then, right from the start so it was a great club. Sensei Len was a great inspiration to me with his tireless enthusiasm for the club and the effort he put into keeping it going, even now over 4 decades later. It was a proper Judo club so we did everything that you normally do, but the influence from Sensei Len and Sensei Derek meant we learned some of the older style of Judo, Kano Jiu Jutsu, which was closer to the Koryu Ju Jutsu origins, so we had a few techniques that wouldn't usually be put into mainstream Judo. They always made sure it was up to each individual however, as to whether you wanted to compete in regional competitions or not.

Judo is starting to change a bit, but you used to have to fight for your grades, they were in two halves. The technique side showing knowledge and understanding, but then also the practical side having to fight for your grades, so you had to win to progress up the belts and that's the way it was always done. If you didn't win your fights, you didn't go up the grades. As a result of that I got used to fighting people that I didn't know from quite early on. I just really enjoyed it, great atmosphere and that's pretty much the same now 40 years on!

Why did you start to diversify?

The way the class run was a children's class first, followed by an adult class. Myself and a couple of others used to stay after the junior class and watch the seniors. It interested me to see what they were doing and it also meant I had time on my hands, so I would quite often be caught looking through the books of Judo Katas, wanting to find out more about the origins of the sport. When I got to finding out there were punches and kicks as well as strange submission and revival techniques, well that just really got me hooked, so I made the decision around 13 or 14 to try and expand more and find out more about Judo's Ju Jutsu origins. There weren't any clubs in the area teaching ju-jitsu however so I ended up having to go a bit more outside of the area continue my further studies. I was always aware of the difference between the martial side and the art side, the self defence side and the sport side and became a bit of a martial geek researching all I could, spending hours and hours in the library reading up on and making notes about the history and lineage of the art, plus associated texts on philosophy and strategy which were also an important part of the foundations and so began my search for that solid link between the samurai and the new modern sport of Judo.

I knew there was a link having seen how the 2 main styles responsible for the founding knowledge of Judo were Kito Ryu Ju Jutsu and Tenjin Shinyo Ryu Ju Jutsu which Kano studied and taught before founding his own style which later became Kodokan Judo. Problem was, trying to find someone teaching these old, Samurai styles in the modern era of Judo, Karate and Kung Fu was next to impossible, or at least it was for someone too young to drive! So I went about trying to learn the different technique ranges contained within these old styles in an attempt to try and gain a better understanding of what the original system felt like, hence studying so many different styles: punches, kicks, pressure points, throws, holds, locks, chokes, strangles, meditation, revival and weapons techniques.

I was always aware of the ability to use Judo for self defence and we trained like that too. The older juniors trained with all the adults and it helped you to get an idea of what it would be like to meet that kind of resistance in real life. The first time I had someone try and stab me for real in the street was when I was 14 too and my training came in pretty handy there. Had I not had training, the story might have been very different and I might not be here now. In fact, I know I wouldn't be as, whilst I had successfully defended against being stabbed, close range in the chest with no warning and managed to walk away having 'taken possession' of the knife, when I later got changed at home, I found a small red dot of blood right in the middle of my solar plexus where the tip of the blade touched just as I got to it - it happened that fast and was that close.

I went on to study Karate & Kickboxing to learn more about the striking, and Aikijujitsu and aikido for the immobilization, locking and throwing side. I eventually went into Kyusho Jutsu/Atemi Jutsu to learn about the pressure points and associated principles and also studied Japanese Reiki, meditation and some of the traditional weapons such as Bo staff, Jo staff, Sai, Kama, Nunchaku, Tonfa, Sword, Jutte and Fan, so studied as much as I could to piece it together. It has probably taken me the best part of around 30 years to get close to my technical ideal and then 3 years ago, I eventually found someone who teaches the art that I wanted to study all those years ago, Tenjin Shinyo Ryu Ju Jutsu, near Southend-On-Sea. Not just anyone either. Shike Paul Masters, Menkyo Kaiden. He has full transmission of all the teachings making him the only non-Japanese person to receive this grade in Tenjin Shinyo Ryu in its entire history. He had been teaching a private group of students for a long time, was licensed directly by the highest Japanese authority and was keen to speak to likeminded Martial Artists who wanted to study and preserve the teachings of the style. So I contacted him, had a few online discussions with his eldest son, Lee Masters, Menkyo, and set up a meeting. Since then, every 6 weeks I do a 5 hour round trip to learn under him at the Hombu Dojo with

Salvatore de Francisci, one of my long suffering students. Now learning under Shike, my training has finally started in earnest!

When did you decide to go out on your own and set up your own place then?

When I was about 16, training in Judo, Kung Fu, Karate and Kickboxing and doing all my other research on various aspects of Ju Jutsu, I formulated what I wanted to do in my own syllabus. I'd written it all down, the aspects that I wanted to study and techniques I wanted to work on for myself and kind of put things back together again to get back to the original system I wanted. I still have the hand written notes somewhere for my syllabus and eventually I got to the point where there was a grading structure and a system of progression as it were. It took me probably around another 8 years from there to really solidify it and get it to a place where it was workable. At that point I was already a 1st or 2nd Dan in Aikijujitsu and I then had a word with a guy who was very well known at the time called Soke Brian Dossett, the head of Spirit Combat International. He gave me the confidence to go out on my own and start a club with my own syllabus. I ran through everything with him, Master Richard Hopkins head of WUMA and many other top organisations and they were fully behind it, backed me and again, I never looked back!

Where I was living and teaching, there were no Ju Jutsu clubs and there never had been any so mine was the first in the area, an area I knew really well. All the other clubs I had trained with over the years were behind me 100%, apart from the fact that my Kung Fu Sifu wanted me to give up everything else and concentrate only on Kung Fu! I had a few of the guys come down and see what we were doing and it just grew from strength to strength. The Japanese style of Ju Jutsu was very popular when it first came over in the 1890s, hugely so. Even Sir Arthur Conan-Doyle wrote about it in the Sherlock Holmes books. So popular was Ju Jutsu in fact, that Edward William Barton Wright who had seen and brought the teachings and some instructors over to the UK from Japan, was able to set up a full time dojo in the heart of London's Piccadilly...... just think what the rates would be today for that! But then Karate and Judo became popular in the 1950's/60s and eclipsed everything else. In the 70s Kung Fu was all the rage with the Bruce Lee mania and that eclipsed everything else at that time. The smaller clubs dotted around the country doing Ju Jutsu struggled a bit in those times, but the people running them would have kept running them even with just one student. So it never really died out completely but it did get extremely quiet. Nowadays it's almost the opposite with BJJ coming in.

How do you feel about the current state of martial arts in general?

It really depends on the circles you travel in as to your experiences. On the whole, and this won't win me many friends, I think the standard is pretty low in this country to be honest. I think there are a few key people who are really doing a lot of work to try and repair that and build it back up. It's not a slight on those people at all, as they're doing good work trying to build the standard back up, but it is an acknowledgement of the fact that a few years back people were starting to realise that, 'maybe I can start my own club and earn lots of money'. People were doing it without the expertise, experience or knowledge and so whilst they are really concerned about getting lots of people in the door, they weren't as concerned with the standard. That's driven the standard down in that sense and there's a lot of that mindset still in this country. Thankfully though, there are a group of very good, very motivated instructors around the UK who are trying to repair that loss, some have been around for decades, plugging away in the background at the good stuff, others are new in but have been trained properly and so that's really good and we should do all we can to support them. It's an important thing and it has to be done right. It's kind of like learning how to drive from someone who has never sat in a car before, let alone driven one - it's important to have people there with the right experience and knowledge. But even then, they need the right know-how of how to teach and transmit it effectively. Being able to do it yourself doesn't mean you can teach it to someone else so you have to have both sides.

Do you separate the terms of self defence and martial arts?

It comes down to words at the end of the day! People use a particular word to describe something but it doesn't really make a difference to the content. The same words can be used to describe two different things. Someone might use the term martial arts to describe a Koryu - old school traditional Japanese martial art, but likewise other people might use the same word for a kickboxing school. To me they're vastly different with different objectives. The word we use in the west of martial means `War` from Mars, the Roman God of War. So, by definition it should be a technique range and application that can be used in a real fighting situation where there are no rules, so in that sense its closer to real self defence than a fighting sport which has many rules. But today, many people use the term martial art to describe any fighting form of sports, but they are completely different things. It doesn't mean necessarily, that one can't be used for the other, but you just have to know how to adapt it.

A lot of the guys who have studied traditional martial arts, I'm one of them, never go out to get into fights as that's not what they're about. But if you're convinced you're learning 'self-defence' yet never have your stuff pressure tested, how do you know it will actually work? There's the age old argument of the traditionalist numpty saying they don't do competitions as their techniques are too dangerous and they might kill someone!! Rubbish!! Then the other side is from the sports side, many of whom say they do competition because it shows how good their stuff is under real pressure and more recently, some are validating the authenticity of what they do by claiming 'ancient' self-defence ancestry. They are both unwittingly using each other to validate what they do and claim one is better than the other. But, fighting under lots of rules, or not fighting at all, is no real preparation for fighting with NO rules! They are different. They should just accept what they do and be good at what they do and that's it! There is validity and usefulness in both methods.

I classify them slightly differently. A martial art is designed for combat in times of war when you might have to take someone's life to protect your own. I also teach combat ju jitsu as well, which is a sports based version that's been running for almost 30 years. Although there are some similar techniques, the objectives are completely different. I'm reminded of that James Bond film where they face off for a fight and as the first Japanese guy bows, James Bond kicks him in the nuts! Don't bring the wrong set of rules to the wrong fight. People mix the names up though and it gets very confusing and grey!

If you teach self defence do you think you need to have real life experience?

I think it depends on the how it is transmitted. You could have someone who has learnt from someone who has had all the experience and if they are able to translate those experiences over well to others, then it could be effective. At the end of the day, we have to be able to say that it's a system that is taught - not everyone teaching it will have had that real life experience, because in order to make them do that is to say 'come on our course, learn it, then go to the pub and get in as many fights as you can!' It's not as easy as that and some of us that have had that experience have had it not because we've looked for it, but because we have had no other choice - it's happened upon us and we've had to use whatever we can do to get through it.

If you've been lucky - or unlucky enough to have had that experience, it kind of allows you to look at how you can adapt what you've learnt. You can't just take stuff straight out of a kata in the dojo onto the street without knowing that you might have to change or adapt something. It's that fluidity of your mental capacity to change, as and when you have to, sometimes with no notice, which is what separates people who have and haven't had experience. Real experience should give you access to that mental switch which allows you to go into 'flipmode' fast, aggressive, violent movement as soon as it is switched. The problem some people have is that they then don't know how to switch that off and go overboard which is when they then get into trouble. It's having the ability to get to that switch whenever you need to and then choosing when to switch it on and off which is more difficult to teach than any physical technique! You have to find other ways to put that across to people such as animal days, pressure testing or physical combat, which try and help test what you're learning to see how you react to the pressure. But also mental preparation, analysis and emotional training is just as important and a lot of clubs don't teach that.

It's the instructor with the experience, who has to legitimately pass the information on and put their students in a situation where they feel pressure and see if they can come up with the goods. Otherwise it's just untested theory and the worst time to find out it doesn't work is when you have to really use it. It's too late then!

The first thing that really made me look at things differently was when I was 14 and had someone try and stab me. It was a weird moment as it was face to face, there was no gesturing, none of the normal sort of trigger factors you'd look for. It just happened really quick. I managed to defend or I wouldn't be here as when I get home and took my top off I noticed the red pin prick that was right by my heart where the blade had touched before I moved. I managed to get off the line, take him to the floor, control the knife and take it off him, but that would have easily severed my aorta so I was really lucky! When I look back on what I did then with the knowledge I have now, I think it was too slow! But I was lucky, by that point, 7 years training, I'd already got ideas of moving my body off the centre line and taking control so that really did help to shape how I looked at things.

Much later on I fell into door work after a friend asked me to help out saying, "yes okay I'll help out", and then 21 years later I finally retired from the door! I never planned to do it at all, certainly not for that long anyway, but just fell into it! I just carried on doing it, but am really glad I did do it, as it gave me the opportunity to technically use a lot of the stuff we teach. There were a lot of fights over that time. I've never been one of those people who will stand there and be like, I've had over 300 fights and done this and that, as it's just stroking the ego as far as I'm concerned, it's not what I'm about. I had a job to do and I was good at doing it. I didn't need external validation from anyone else because, if I was crap at it, I'd have woken up in the hospital, several times!

Working on the door for me was looking at body language and trigger factors, trying to stop the trouble before it starts, building a rapport with the customers, looking after the staff, being a first aider and an Agony Uncle all wrapped up into one, as well as looking at the technical knowledge of physical restraint and self defence. That knowledge gave me the confidence to get stuck in when I needed to, as I knew there were always options to control a rising scale of physicality at my disposal. The guys who weren't training, all they could do was punch, so in a sense they were just on an even par with everyone else. They might be big and strong, but unless they're trained, they still can't punch. Everyone believes they have the ultimate knockout punch, until they test it! It gave me the chance to try lots of different things and every technique in my syllabus, the core kihons, I've used for real so I know that they work and I've tested them. I didn't go in to work with a tick list in a little black book and go, right tonight I'm doing this technique, it's just what works at the time so you have to train to have an answer for lots of different situations. They all worked at the time in real fights, so I quite happily stand by those techniques as I've physically had to use them and some of my students have become door staff and had to use them too. They've stood the test of time and it's still going 22 years later.

What are your thoughts on the business and martial arts mix then?

I don't see anything wrong with making a business or living out of martial arts, the same as any other industry. For those that do, if they're doing it for the right reasons and are teaching quality and with integrity, it can be the best thing in the world as most of the people trying to do that, you would assume, are doing it because they love it. You don't go to the job centre and they give you a self defence instructor course to start up your own club purely for an income, but if people do that, they don't enjoy it as they're in it for the wrong reasons. The only problem I have is with the ones with no experience or integrity, doing it purely for profit and scamming people out of money, giving them crap in return. A lot of companies now use the pyramid type scheme where you are trained and branch out on your own, then you train others to branch out and so on. That's the usual order of many businesses. The problem comes when they're not passing down the knowledge or experience in what they're teaching and making people pay more money for it. Any other industry, they'd be done under the trade descriptions act as by the time it's filtered down to the people paying the money, they aren't actually learning what they're paying for. There's no substance to what they're learning, thus showing the people at the top have no integrity. They may have had knowledge to start with, just not wanting to pass it on, but I'm a firm believer that they just didn't have the knowledge in the first place or weren't trusted enough to run their own organisations. They're the only people I have a problem with doing it.

We martial artists as a community should be doing whatever we can do, to be able to highlight these problems as many members of the public don't realise it. Not just the punters, but the schools hosting the clubs or the sports centres hiring their premises, they should be aware that these people aren't actually qualified to do it. You can go on the internet nowadays and be a 13th Dan in a couple of hours, there has to be a way of maintaining the standards and integrity within our industry. When we can do that legitimately, as a whole community or industry, instead of all the futile political squabbling, we'll have a much better system which will benefit loads of people. I'm all for tidying it up and getting rid of the idiots, but there seems to be quite a few! I think that is starting to happen for the right reasons with the group of great instructors coming through that I referred to earlier, but there are still some idiots rising to a high media platform in martial arts who shouldn't be there at all!

The quality people just want to teach the knowledge and regardless of what style they come from, you often find they all look very similar if being applied by someone who knows what they're doing and has also had real experience. When I see a great instructor like Gavin Mulholland teaching Karate, to me it looks like Ju Jutsu. That's not to say one is better than the other, it's more like a physical *Namaste* to say that 'the truth of one recognises the truth of the other'.

Steve Rowe was very vocal about this sort of thing when he spoke of getting rid of all the style names in martial arts as, at the end of the day it's compartmentalising everything and it gets very confusing when people use the wrong names. Ultimately, true technique is true regardless of the name you give it. If it works, it works. If I punch someone on the jaw and KO them, the fact that it works does not depend on whether I use the word seiken, Stomach 5 or Banana, as long as you can remember where I taught you to strike, that's what's important. People confuse names or use the wrong ones and that's where it gets very confusing, especially for new starters.

What has martial arts done for you and what can do it do for people?

We have a program for children, mainly in schools, called SD3 – Self Defence, Self Discipline and Self Development. 3 of the main areas I believe martial arts excels at with both children and adults alike. I've certainly gained a great deal of confidence, personal and spatial awareness, self defence skills and social opportunities from martial arts over the years, but one of the most important things we ask when new people come, is what they want from the training. It's something people forget about. There might be some spiel or sales patter that is given, but ultimately it's what the individual wants out of it themselves which is important, because you'll get out of it what you put in. If you're enthusiastic, you're going to get more out of it in return if it's done properly. People do it for different reasons and that has to be respected. Some do it for self defence if they've have bullying issues or something, others want it to compete and test their skills that way. Some just want to learn the history and culture and it's all cool! That's one of the good things we get out of martial arts as a generic form, in that there are so many facets to it. The problem comes when the instructor doesn't ask or care what the individual wants or forces them down a path they don't want to go down. It has to be tailored to the individual. The fundamentals are there for everyone but once they've learned that, you should be able to see which area people are more suited to. If that means they have to go and seek guidance from someone else, then that's fine and we shouldn't be holding them back and making them prisoner to our school! You're helping them on a journey but you don't know where that path will go until you go a certain way down it, so just help how you can.

Different arts suit different people. We have different strengths, weaknesses, ranges of movement and flexibility as well as motivations to study in the first place, so it might take several attempts before a new student finds a system which they feel comfortable enough to work within. Today, most people think of BJJ when you mention Ju Jitsu. But, there are many different styles of Ju Jitsu. Each style expresses some part of the form known as Ju Jitsu. Some are predominantly sport, some self defence and some are historically important to Japan, having hailed from the Samurai era. You wouldn't describe Milkshake solely by using the word Banana. Milkshake is the form, Strawberry, Chocolate, Banana or Vanilla are all flavours or styles of the form known as Milkshake. So BJJ, Kito Ryu, Kodokan Judo, Aikido and Mizu Ryu are flavours or styles of the form known as Ju Jitsu. Don't mistake one individual flavour as defining the whole form. Each has its merits but individually contain only one, or a few component parts of the whole form.

What is important is to try a few and find the flavour that you like the most. But remember, banana milkshake from MaccyD's will taste different to banana milkshake from M&S, so once you've found the flavour you like, remember, each outlet (club) will have its own way of mixing those ingredients that is unique to them. Find the flavour you like and stick with it long enough to appreciate all the ingredients that go into making it what it is and true to what you need or want.

Leading on from that then, what makes a good instructor?

Experience aside, one of the key things I think is being fluent enough to change. If you teach in groups, not everyone will learn at the same speed or understand the way that you're putting it across, just like in normal education. A group of kids in a class with one teacher who has to get a certain amount of info across in an hour. The pace goes to the teacher, not necessarily the individuals. We have the ability in martial arts to tailor tuition to individuals and identify when someone needs to be taught in a different manner and that's what we should be doing. We should be fluent enough to change our teaching habits to cater for those individuals. It's an individual thing so one of the key qualities is just being able to pay attention to the individuals you're teaching and help them learn in the best way possible. If it's not being picked up properly, it might not be the student's fault; you need to find a new way to deliver the information so they can pick it up.

Another aspect forgotten or not even thought about by many is, as the head of a club, you have put yourself in the target range. There

MARTIAL MASTERS Vol 1

are people out there; I've had a couple over the years, who relish in turning up to a club and joining in with the express intention to argue, disagree and generally cause havoc, even escalating things to physical confrontation. So, if you're advertising yourself as the premier self protection instructor in the county, you best be able to back up your statements or, when push comes to shove, you might well be losing students as well as losing face.

I'm a nice guy. I'm good at being nice. I'm also good at being bad. I don't take intimidation or threats kindly, but I'm always willing to share techniques with people, the easy way, or the hard way!

As Dave Courtney likes to say:

"It's nice to be important, but it's more important to be nice".

Russell Jarmesty
Jarmesty Martial Arts Academy

Russ Jarmesty is the lead instructor at Jarmesty Martial Arts Academy in Atherton. A Manchester lad born and bred who started with Karate and after hitting the doors realised he needed something to change so started to look at Jiu-Jitsu. He was lucky enough to have found Trev Roberts who had already been in the game for 30 odd years and so started to look at the `no fluff` martial arts. After 15 years on the doors and 20 years teaching martial arts, Russ now runs his full time academy and is considered one of the leading reality based instructors in the country having recently won `Reality Instructor of the Year` at the British Martial Arts Awards.

Let's start at the beginning then. Why martial arts? When? Why?

To start with the martial arts, I never needed it. I was already fighting, already scrapping and I'd never lost a fight. I was an angry kid which was mint! I didn't get into martial arts to learn to fight, or for confidence or spiritual stuff, a friend of mine was training and was having a few scraps legally so I thought all the shit I get in trouble for outside, he gets rewarded for! He's doing stuff and getting belts so I thought I'd have a bit of that! I knew nothing about the karate side so I saw it and to me it just looked like the film side so I thought I'd give it a go. Looking back I didn't like about 90% of what we were doing, give me the sparring day and that's where it was for me. Friday was always Kumite and my mate Darren was the only guy I could really get stuck in with, the rest weren't having it so I'd say the club, thinking about it was more of a non-contact club. The instructor just left us alone to knock bells out of each other. That's how we got started with it. I loved it, still do, but it was useless in the form we were doing it in. It was very rigid with kata and the only thing I liked about that was the stances. I have a strong head and the stances seemed very strong so when you sank down and locked the move in, I loved that side of it. But then the softer side for me just didn't cut it.

In the world of martial arts there's a little hint of lavender running through everything and a little bit of campness going on. The way I look at it, everything is one thing with the martial arts. You look at the kicks and punches then call it kickboxing, then look at some throws and it's Judo. Every little sector starts dragging it to their side and saying `that's mine now`. Martial arts are everyone's. Krav Maga is pretty prominent at the moment and so when I do things people say `Oh that's Krav`. It isn't, it's the jiu-jitsu I learnt but at the end of the day it's just martial arts. We can't forget that martial arts are two separate words `martial` and `art`. I already had the martial head where I'd die on the battlefield if I had to and it was a pleasure for me when I was younger. The art side, that was the study for me, it was getting the fluency of it, but again I was a natural fighter so it was just a bolt-on. I never needed the martial arts, I really didn't, I just legally got to have good scraps with people and I was in a world where I just wanted more stuff to hurt people with. I can't lie and say I did it because I wanted to make myself better because at that point, give me something that fucking hurts them or stops them hurting me! That was the search and that's why the jiu-jitsu came in and training with Trev. If you've ever trained with Trev, he uses a line regularly "I won't take liberties" and the next minute it's like fucking hell! What the fuck! But it's not taking liberties; it would be if he didn't put it on as you wouldn't appreciate it. Once you felt it you'd be like `Ah I'll have that Trev, I know exactly where that bastard will fit`. So routines, I was never arsed about them, give me the gold that hurts.

How did you first meet Trev?

I knew Trev as a family friend. My mother left our house when we were 15 and moved to Bolton with Trev's right hand man on the doors, so she lived with John for a long time and that's how I met Trev. He ran all the doors in Bolton and used to go to his pub. He's heavily involved in rescue staffies and we love staffies so every time the dog would come in we'd look after it. I knew Trev and what he did but never trained with him. After the karate finished, I was looking around and thought let's get to Trev's place, especially as the door work had started. He broke the mould for me, and I always knew him, but I started training in the 90's with him which the karate club didn't like as there was a cross over and they said I had to just train with them! It was great leaving that club as we had a bit of an argument and I bit back, then it was almost like he kicked me out of the club. This is where the smoke screen disappeared as soon as I left, I was out of the club and he told me to get out of the car park. I then suggested he get out of the car park before I kicked the living fuck out of him because I was angry and I saw his eyes change. He realised he didn't have the control he had over me that you do as an instructor to a student and I was now just a guy stood in front of him. I saw this guy that I had looked up to for five years turn into this little quibbling wreck and then I got even more upset. I'd been blindly riding off this guy since the day I walked in but could have leathered him the day I walked in! My martial arts were for martial and I laid faith in my instructor and faith in myself but we all fuck up. I realised we all fuck up and it's a fairly common thing so we have to be okay with that and just be happy being us. I'm happy being me and that's it.

When we start teaching the martial arts, I teach something and say `lay your faith in this it works`, but then other stuff I'll say don't, it won't. You need to be able to hold onto something, but then let it go just as easily. It's always better to let go of something than to have it ripped from you and so when I saw that instructor's arse drop at the thought of me smacking him I knew this just wasn't what I needed or wanted to be. He was nothing. He had such an attitude where we should be bowing down and praying to him and then you go and meet Trev who is exactly he. There's no ego, he's just a dead nice guy who loves training. From my first when I stepped in I just though what the fuck have I been doing with that Karate. I loved it so didn't deny it, I just realised that that instructor didn't know anything. He had the moves, that's all and he probably read them from the book. Trev had the head so my job then was to take the martial arts to the streets and see where they fit.

Let's talk about your times on the doors then as a `Brutal Bouncer`

One of the main questions is did your martial arts work on the door? It did and it didn't but there's a very prominent day where I fought and remember thinking that I have a responsibility. I tried my best to make the punch work, a clean reverse punch on this nobhead in front with two of his monkey mates at the side. He was gobbing off a bit and being held back but then broke free and ran through so I yakazuki'd him, nice reverse punch to the head and he did something that no one else has ever done when I've hit them – he didn't go down. Everyone I hit goes down! It was a clean snap hit, pull back and he just stumbled back a bit! I don't pull back anymore, when I hit I want to go clean through your head and see the brains dripping out the back! It won't happen but that's the intention behind the punch. The guy I hit didn't go down and so for me, my martial arts didn't work at that point. I have a luxury however of just going back to the old me and scrapping. As soon as he didn't go down, his balls just got bigger and his two mates just decided that they're now on his side so they come too. I've just gone back to being me at this point, dropped the first guy, picked him up, pushed another one off and caught the original guy with a front kick which I will credit with Karate. I've got an evil front kick and it's been practiced for far too long. He's sat down and I'm having a scuffle with his mates again. This guy I'd just kicked is now getting up off the floor and I can't afford to let that happen so the nearest thing was his head, and the nearest weapon was my foot so they met. But that made a real fucking mess of the guy. I'm not interested in whether he got hurt or not as we're all responsible for our own shit when it goes off but then when I got home the next morning, I got shit at home! I'm not in this game to get shit; I get paid for getting it at work but not at home! I had blood all over me and she asked me what happened so like an idiot I told her. Then she looked at me like she was disgusted and just said to me "you said you'd never kick anyone in the head" but I didn't have a choice! The guy was getting back up and if he had, that was me done. She was disgusted with me and we split up for a year after I started doing the doors as, rightly so, she didn't like the person I was changing into. I'd always been that person; she just didn't get to see it as often. So I thought, hang on Russ if that punch had worked I wouldn't have had to kick him in the head, so I have a responsibility to stop things escalating where I can. That was a wake up moment where if you hit someone, make them go down as I have a responsibility for my own safety but also theirs as he wouldn't have had to have his face rewired if that initial punch had just worked. So I realised make sure they always go down, and take spare clothes with you!

Getting on the doors was through Trev really. I broke my neck on a training session with him which put me out of action for 18 months. That also meant no tournaments for me as I couldn't risk it so I went into door work. I worked 5-6 nights a week so a full time door man, I'd train in the morning and afternoon then straight on the doors at night. I jacked in after 15 years on a Saturday after a great party then on the Sunday I was excited as was going to be building the academy and wanted to get started. Around the 3 month mark it was hurting my head. I'd not seen anyone or been out, had been sleeping at the academy and suddenly thought this is fucking hard work! I went and saw my mate Lee back on the door in town and asked how things were so he said he'd had a bit the night before and gave me the details then asked what I'd been up to and I was like "errrr, David's getting on with Gail in Corrie, and milk costs £1.67 a tub mate". That was the big fucking difference, I was turning into a day walker stood at the shop waiting to buy my milk. That's never been me, you guys wake up in the morning and I'm sleeping. I wake up just before dark and that was the biggest difference, the excitement to queuing for milk! I got ill building this and my hair fell out with alopecia so I thought it's time to reassess as I'm a fighter and like fighting. Everyone has their drug and mine was fighting. I loved it from the argument to the feeling I got and I lost that for a while and starting getting angrier. Road rage would come in and I thought I need to sort this or everyone is going to suffer.

6 months after that I'm back at the doors saying hello to all the staff just having a chat and they had a bit of a scuffle which to me was a very basic incident then the girls start coming out and asking where the toilets are while they're scrapping and to me at that point, I was cured. I didn't miss it anymore and then thought, right I'm definitely not a door man anymore.

What's your opinion on the reality-based self defence world at the moment?

You always get the petty little lavender arguments that go if you haven't had a fight, you shouldn't be teaching self defence. People get annoyed by this and go, oh well if you've never had a boxing fight, should you be teaching boxing? That's a sport, there's a luxury where you get to analyse the guy you're going to be fighting and get a game plan for him. A good eye for that sport and craft, you don't have to be a fighter. But in my world, it's simple. I can give you every technique I've got but it means fuck all if someone comes up to you, your arse starts going and you can't implement any of that bag of tools I've given you as you're too scared. I had the routines down but every time I tried applying it the way it was shown I had to go back to kicking the guy in the head and just going back to being a nasty bastard stamping on them. I'm an analyser and I went on the doors to study. I never let the karate go, I just thought maybe I did it wrong, so went in with a blank head and though I'd try stuff, if I ended up on my arse, so be it. If you've never had a fight and just have routines, that's not self defence, it's an art form. If you're able to say to people listen guys this stuff works, but I'm also going to show you how it doesn't work, and what you need to make sure of is not losing your head if it doesn't work, you just carry on. We've already had a fuck up as we're fighting so they'll probably be another fuck up. The difference I sussed out years ago is being comfortable. I would get guys in positions I was comfortable with on the street, but there was always one maybe that something wouldn't work on. Then for a split second you get a doubt going what now? So in that moment, I just twat them... I never have that moment where I think shit, then end up in the shit. There's a confidence shift if something doesn't work, but if you let it show, his confidence goes up massively and yours drops.

If you had to train someone for 1 hour to have a fight with a proper nasty bastard, what would you teach? Not a single fucking technique is going to work at that point just for an hour is it? So I'd go, even before I started doors I was a fighter and I've already been beaten so can't be beaten any more in my head, physically or emotionally. If I have a guy for an hour, I'd get a hypnotist in and get them to hypnotise them to say they're the hardest fucker in the world and no one can touch them. You're immune to pain and don't understand quitting. That fucker will be difficult to beat, even if he only has a jab and a cross. I know who I am and have proved it, when I'm fighting I'm the hardest fucker imaginable and I can't lose. I just have a certain set mentality that allows it. I teach that by getting people to see the light slowly over a period. I don't teach techniques to start; I show you where your head goes. We have to know how to work our way around emotions. If you're teaching self defence and all you have is routines, I promise you its shit, you need to teach that emotional connection. This is done by pressure testing which is the ultimate test really! It brings knowledge and understanding of what needs to be done. You need to lose the niceness as martial artists are supposed to be calm nice people, but that's the last thing I'm going to be if we get in to it, you're going to feel stuff! We can't deny our emotions, we accept them so I know I have a few demons, but I don't get rid of them, I pet them and feed them, they're mine for when I need them.

I looked up to the guys I trained with and each one had pure respect and a history to them. You could trace it and see where they came from and where the respect came from. So I thought, I needed to have a history and 15 years work on the doors will give me that history. I'll keep teaching the karate and jiu-jitsu but I'll never let someone think they've just done one session and they can therefore now kill someone. I wanted the history and was willing to put myself on the line for it. I see now, the 3 month courses, the 3 week courses where you get a certificate and suddenly you're opening a club up next door to me?!

What's the state of the martial arts in your opinion today then?

There are so many different flavours. I'm a simple man and I love simplicity. I've got a guy who teaches yoga and inner peace, well he better be a fucking peaceful man hadn't he?! If someone cuts him up in the road and he gets angry, it's like hang on you conning little bastard, you're meant to be this inner peace guy! If you're a fighter who teaches street fighting, but never had a fight, maybe you're missing a key ingredient? You can't read about that ingredient, you just have to get in it, there's no other way of doing it. If you say you're a World Champion, show me your medals, I'm simplistic like that. The way martial arts fall down now in my opinion is the instructors who think they're something they're not. I'm Russ, I'm sat here with a fag in my hand, I do what I do, but to the kids I'm a god and I understand that. I don't play up to it, I destroy it straight away and say if you want to be like me, not everything as it's a weird place in my head. But if you want to be as good at fighting as me, I'll give you the keys because I trained a lot and gave it all. Some people are in the room, but their head's aren't, they're just going through the motions. The barriers need to be broken down between student and instructors, there's no difference, and we're just good at what we do. People hide behind certificates and won't test what they do, thinking the pleasures in life come from seeing a kid walk out of class with a new certificate in their hands. The pleasure for me comes from when I tell the kids to do something deliberately wrong, and a few will question it when others will just piss around for half an hour knowing it's wrong. They're the ones strong enough to stand up for themselves. Understand being yourself, and in a fight you need to fight, tap into that place where you can nail it and get inside your own head, knowing you're the biggest, baddest person ever!

I'm not proficient in every martial art so can't really talk but for me it just goes down to, does it work? Give me a guy for 3 months and at the end he has to have a fight. Does he fare better than he did before, or has he just got a bag of tricks he can't use, creating a scared black belt. The grades in our style up to blue belt go on the art and the nice moves. By blue, your head goes into a place where it becomes the martial. We say to the kids, your parents will ask what you've been doing; show us something so show them this. Its movie stuff they'll be impressed. But at blue we say, get them to hold their arms out, which they will as you've asked them to, then just wait for a sec and punch them in the nuts. Why are you stood there with your arms out to the side? It's sort of a head game! Life's a head game as is martial arts. Just be honest with your students and be in it for the right reasons. I teach the kids to be able to protect myself against someone like me and if that kid thinks putting his hands up and asking not to be hit would have stopped me, it wouldn't. It's like paying back; I owe society quite a lot from when I was a kid so it's a form of redemption. Kids need to make mistakes as you learn from them, just don't beat yourselves up when you get it wrong. Do that at school, get something wrong and you get a bollocking and told you're stupid, you're not stupid, and you just got it wrong which we've all done. Fall over, get back up. Lose the fear of fighting, and you can only do that through fighting. People get upset and offended by what I say, but I don't give a fuck. You should be offended and feel what it's like, then figure out why you're offended, what are you holding on to so much that you can be offended with it? Learn to let it go, just like your martial arts.

I love the offending side as only the egotistical ones get titsy about it, the rest will throw their opinions in and suddenly we have a discussion which is great! I've been pissed off many a time, a lot more than the guy teaching who I say that won't work mate and I'll show you why. I love being proved wrong and love being proved right! I have that much freedom in my head I don't give a shit. If it works, have it, if it doesn't why do we train it? Well for the movement, the fitness and maybe one day it will help a little. Most martial arts are babysitting clubs and are desperate to keep them even if they're not bothered about being there but the instructor barely knows their name. I want to know the kids and why they're here. Please the parents please the kids and see what they want from the martial arts. How can you not have a connection with all your students? If you do, money means nothing. We obviously need to make a living but there are too many schools out there that see martial arts as just a cash cow to get rich quick.

You need to make it real and have the experience to make it real. Every attacker has a dream in their head and know what they want to do, I've seen it 1000 times. You know when the attacker is going to attack, and his dream in his head is to smash the fuck out of you. He says something, you respond something like "come on then" as soon as he says "you want some". I turn it around and say sorry mate, do I want what? I deviate slightly from his plan. Every step of the way his dream of what is going to happen gets stopped by me. I'll admit I've been a dick, I haven't but I'm lying, its martial arts, it's deceitful you outflank and play mind games. Then, bam, I give him a slap. He was about to go for me, I slap, it ends. I pacify people, then twat them! If they then go for the fight they need to be careful as I don't let them choose the rules at that point. When we first started on the doors we were fighting every night. But as we got more and more experienced, we got into less and less, do you think the town changed, or I did? I don't see people gobbing off at me as big threats anymore, I'm not scared, I just smashed the fuck out of them. After a while I realise people aren't big threats, they're something I can play with as my confidence was through the roof. That was the fun time, when I could play with them, know they were lined up for a shot and take it. The three stages of my training were the shit stages where I'd just kick the fuck out of them, then it was the play stage where I knew what I was doing. Then finally came the stage where it was like, do you really want this, because you're going to get hurt. I just saw the guy as a victim and wanted to know what was going on. I'd suggest going round and having a ciggy, then if they wanted to fight after, fair play, but after the cig. We'd have a chat and normally it was something like their missus had had a go, shit day etc.

Talk to us about your experience in teaching then

I teach around 200 kids every week, I'm a full time instructor with Zach. I can get a kid in and see they've got older brothers, as they're scrappy little bastards! If you've got an older brother, rough and tumble shit is a regular occurrence and you get that fighting spirit. Some of the exercises we do is simply to push someone else off the mat. It gives them that fighting spirit and gets the fire lit.

Sometimes all it takes is a kid to get annoyed then suddenly they're starting to fight back a little more! First they'll get upset and maybe there's a little tear, which isn't a bad thing necessarily. I just ask for an hour of their time, and to trust me, and they'll walk out and will have learnt something from the class. My son when he was 8 years old loved Power Rangers, so I said when you're on the back foot and need some extra strength say to yourself "go go Power Rangers" because he fucking loved them. I could see the moment he said it to himself as they'd be that little extra! Our brains are so much stronger than our bodies and if you can get inside your own head, you'll find strength you'll never knew you had. I trained people with disabilities and they've got madness of strength as they just don't understand the limitations the brain can sometimes put on you. So I get into the kids head and try and give them that extra little bit of strength and go! As Rhys got older, maybe it wasn't "go go Power Rangers" anymore, but it was something like "who the fuck are you to look at me like that and make me feel like that". You've got that head now, so let's look at the art then put the two together and wow, that's something not to mess with. One without the other, it's all a bag of shit. My head makes my stuff work, nothing else. If I punch that punch ball machine, I'm punching it with everything!

I knew that I'd be using the training I was doing during the day that night on the doors so it gave me an extra bit and an extra mentality that a lot of people don't have! I hate running, don't do it, but get me on those mats and I'll fight all day. Say go for a ten minute run and I'll tell you to piss off, I don't run from everyone! Our warm ups are fighting, starting from a hooking in position. I show on seminars, I can get a 5th Dan and a white belt and say to them get round the back of him and put on a choke, it's the white belt's job to stop him. A minute later, has he got round the back? Has he fuck! He looked exactly like the white belt doing it! You're the same but the white belt might just drown a little quicker from a lack of confidence. Get that white belt that doesn't give a fuck about what grade you are and at that point you're fucking fighting! Every couple of months, put a day aside, put some gloves on and scrap. Video it and video the session the week before and tell me where the differences are. Then you can see what you're teaching and can adapt to it more. Fighting in scruffy, we fall and it doesn't look good! 5% of what we do is the street self defence e.g. `Mean Streets` I invested time in that and think I nailed it. We're martial artists though with an underlying tone that it has to work on the street. Wrist locks might not work the way they do in training as you can't get the wrist but if I stick my thumb in someone's eye, they're going to grab my wrist and boom, I'm in! I like the art, I like the martial but everything needs to be tested. I need to know who I am, and I need to know who my students are. Are they fighters, or runners? If they're fighters I teach them to fight. If they're runners I teach them to run. I can see what people are as soon as I put them on the mats. Some will run, some won't ever run no matter who they're up against they'll always fight. Know your students, they all learn differently! We don't really advertise or anything, but we don't lose students. We've become part of the community over 20 years and I don't think there's a single kid in the area who hasn't trained with us at some point or another. They look up to you so we have a responsibility to teach them well. Just be polite!

I was always polite on the doors as I thought if I'm polite it's easier to spot a dickhead! We teach that to the kids, and in a way we teach it to the adults too. Adults sometimes still aren't comfortable in their skin but aren't always. We asked a few months back who wanted to go in for training and have a fight. There was the usual lot doing it then we asked someone a bit newer who was a bit "errrrr ummm", which meant no he didn't want to fight. His mates then started giving him a bit of shit so he was like "yeah alright". I was like hang on, no, you don't want to so don't, and you've just failed your grade and been peer pressured! How old are you! You want to see martial, look at Linda who is a little 54 year old with us, I said to her "next Saturday you want to fight?" She went "Do I hell, but I'll have a brew", she's a martial artist; she's comfortable and can't be peer pressured!

The name of the book is `Martial Masters` and I technically fucking hate that word as it conjures up an image in my head that's negative. I like the word `elders` as they've been around the martial arts a long time, but as soon as someone proclaims to be a master I struggle. What are they masters of? Their art or themselves? If it's the art any monkey could do that and I could probably show a good ballet dancer to look great and master the art as they have the flexibility and strength already. No one is a master, we're all still learning! I've mastered my art and maybe myself but I'm not a master, I'm just Russ. If you want to master an art you have to have passion inside you and really go for it. David Beckham lived and slept with that football and was always the last one kicking it against the wall at night. Discover a passion and go with it! I've spent 20 years teaching now and think I'm a complete instructor, 5 years ago I wasn't, but I knew it and would divert them to the right place. I'm honest, there's no bullshit inside me.

Let's talk about the British Martial Arts Awards then, you were nominated for a number of awards, how did you find it?

Everyone that was nominated for reality based instructor kind of started at the same time and it would have been a great battle to see who would have won it! I am who I am, and I've done what I've done though. It's nice to be appreciated and see people are getting things from me which is my redemption. I grew up reading about some of the guys nominated, but I'm quite dominant on Facebook and always post my shit as if you've got good shit, post it. Lots of people talk a lot but never actually show their stuff. Being up there with those guys did nothing more than prove what I already knew; I'm already on that level with them. I wanted to be sat with them, and I was. It was great to win, but they're all great guys so in a way there were no losers or anything. With the DVD, I would have been insulted if I hadn't won for the simple fact that I don't do anything lightly and I analyse everything I do. It was packaged for someone who really does want self defence. Everything is there for you. There aren't thousands of routines or techniques in there, there's a lot of me talking and some moves but not thousands! Those of you who bought it, it'll probably collect dust and you guys deserve to get battered. Test it, use it, and work it. There hasn't been a single bad review for either the `Mean Streets` app, or the `Brutal Bouncer` boxset, everyone seems to love it which is positive and great for me! I didn't want the name `Brutal Bouncer`, I got a bit screwed into it and Ian won't mind me saying that it was a marketing thing. I wanted to call it `How not to be a dick` or `How to twat dicks`! I'm not a big fan of the title it just makes me seem a bit of a dick but hey it was well received!

The first `Mean Streets` seminar we put on was great because I walked in and the room was filled with some of the top UK martial arts instructors. They weren't students, there were 5th degree black belt guys there, just wanting to train with us. The response was fantastic from everyone as I specialise in this kind of thing and there was a real quality of people in the room, so I went home feeling good! I just needed someone to confirm what I knew to be true and that's where my years on the door helped and this has translated into what I teach on the seminars. I start the seminars by pissing you off, then show you how not to be pissed off. We all work through it together; there are no egos or stuff to hold on to, they're not welcome. It comes down to experience and I have shit loads, I made sure of it. Like I said earlier, everyone I look up to has a background so I made sure I did too. There's ifs or buts with what I teach, I've used it and can give you the date and time when it has been used! I like to give a story behind every technique I teach and it helps to embed into everyone's brains.

What's the future looking like?

There will be a few more DVDs I think. People in my club don't know I have a DVD out, none of them have it! Why do they need it?! They're with me every day! Outside of my club I think people think I'm just a thug, but I'm a martial artist. I'll put my heart out there and try and show that missing link between the traditional martial arts and the street application. You need it, but no fucker has it! The next DVD will be that extra ingredient needed to make it work! That one is going to come out! I'll rename Brutal Bouncer after this year maybe to `How not to be a dick`. Our seminars will keep going as we have a nice little niche of 20 people that regularly come now. It's never a money thing, but it's nice to have a bit of cash. I could rob a bank tomorrow if I wanted money; promise you I could have £1million by tomorrow! The seminars will continue and then that will turn into not an instructors program, but something that I can see people are on the same page as me, rubber stamping someone saying they can speak honestly and truthfully, not necessarily they can fight, but they can speak honestly.

Guardians will continue and again that won't be a money thing apart from with Victoria who puts hours in for it! We first set up Guardians to be truthful and money affects everything so we just want to keep the money out of it! We can't be sold or bent then. We just like to hear about people's journey in the martial arts and what they've been doing.

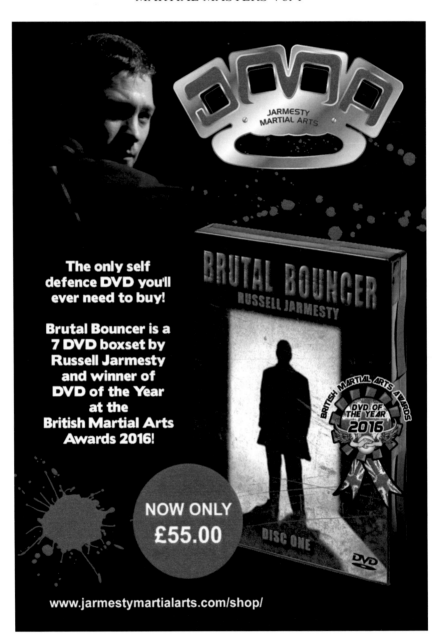

Anthony Pillage
Way of the Spiritual Warrior

Our interview with Tony is a little different, as frankly, Tony is a little different...

Although a revered martial artist who has headlined and sold out SENI, as well as being the owner of the popular Way of the Spiritual Warrior in Coventry, Tony has a bigger story to tell. Those who know him know that the past couple of years have not been easy for him to put it mildly, and this interview for Tony was a way of telling his story and hopefully giving some hope to those who find themselves in a similar position to what he has gone through.

We immensely enjoyed chatting with him in Coventry and hope you enjoy reading his story as much as we enjoyed hearing it.

You've just survived cancer and written a book about it. Can you tell us a little about that?

When I first thought of the idea for the book `Breaking Bob` it was a year ago approximately and what I was thinking was that I would re-hash my old Facebook posts, add a few explanatory paragraphs to it and it would be a pretty nice keep-sake. But over this last year, a lot in my mind has expanded and changed and for the book I wanted to almost explain what that 12 months had done for me. Being given the all clear doesn't mean diddly squat, it just means that there are no tumours at the moment which is obviously a great thing, but I've still got to keep my battle straps tightened as I still have cancer. It would just take that little flick to go back to being shit though! Now I think however, almost from having a full circle from having the cancer diagnosed to having the doctors say they can't find any tumours is that there is a much better story and I've learnt so much about me and life, the universe and everything. I think rather than it just being a sort of token gesture, something that would have validity but wouldn't be brilliant, this could be something that I could make quite extraordinary I think! So I'm taking myself off for a week to some wild coast or somewhere, hiring out a caravan and I'm just going to write until the book is done and done properly as it has a legacy now. It will be an interesting story and I want it to help people who are going through this now. We're supporting 6 people with cancer currently to try and help them and so I see my martial arts taking second place and my helping people with cancer coming forward as my main focus.

The martial arts gave me the strength to fight the fucker and the mentality as that's the main thing. You get that cancer diagnosis and it's like someone sticking an icy dagger in your stomach. I've been very fortunate in that we worked out that up to now I've had 12 depressed and sad bad days which isn't too bad out of the best part of some 400 since the diagnosis. Some of them were very bleak, but there is where the interesting juxtaposition comes in so much that at the end of January I was given 6 months to live. I'd done videos with me sobbing my eyes out, not being able to breath and drugged out on morphine. I thought that was it, and I wasn't going to make it through to the morning and I had that feeling 3 or 4 times where the breathing and the pain just gets too much. But because I went and kept going and didn't give up I have been rewarded hugely so if you look at the last fortnight I've had the best time of my life.

Just take the UK Martial Arts Awards and how good that was! When we put the idea up and were getting people to nominate, it became very clear that people wanted me to win the `Man of the Year` Award, it was quite an emotional thing. I didn't want people to think in any way, shape or form, that this was my awards ceremony and therefore I should win something so that's why I put up every single nomination that was received. I think at the end I had 178 nominations, and the next person down had 6. Some people such as Steve Rowe said I shouldn't accept it, which is fair enough, but then others like Eddie Quinn etc. said go for it. When I got that standing ovation, it was the only standing ovation apart from Jacob's Phelps - the young man with Down's Syndrome who had recently received his Black Belt. I can't tell you how much that meant to me, in the back of my mind there was still that though that people might think I had just got it due to it being my awards – it was my own insecurity. But that spontaneous show of love and support was something incredible and I'll never forget it.

You go from the depths of abject despair which I had to winning the Pride of Coventry Award which was fantastic, and then a few days later, the Muslim School of Coventry that I work with had done a montage about me to congratulate me on getting over the cancer. That was better than anything! Then of course, the day after I go out and meet Wilko Johnson who has now said he'll foreword my book! He's one of my all-time heroes and it was almost like the universe had gifted me something.

The point of me being in this book is not about my martial arts qualifications, it's about my life qualifications and I think that's the really important thing. It's about radiating good things for people. I like helping people, it's what I do and through that I've been rewarded. You look at what happens tonight at the MAI awards, as far as I know I've not seen anyone of particular note going except Alfie Lewis, I could be wrong. But you see the invites printed on shit paper and the names pencilled in! It's wrong! Where's the resonance and meaning in that? It doesn't have any! For me, as long as we've covered our costs I'm happy as it's done for the right reasons. I see my job as educating people in the holistic side of cancer treatment now as the 1939 Cancer Act precludes any holistic treatment at all, but now I'm less cancer sensitive I now have to adjust my diet a little more, take less supplements etc. - but it will give me the time to help other people.

When they found my cancer it was the size of a grapefruit and had grown into the heart wall and into the plural stacks outside the lung. But where the main danger was in my opinion was that it had wrapped itself round my phrenic nerve which is what they had to cut which basically means my right lung is now gone. They cut out around 93% of it, so 7% of it was left but that was growing in an area round the other phrenic nerve so I had to take the option of do I radiate? Chemotherapy was never offered to me. If it's specific they will try to radiate, chemo is spread around. At that time, it hadn't spread and that's what the concern was so much recently with the pain I was getting where they thought they had found a growth on my plural sack which was just a thickening caused by the radiation. To give you an idea of radiation, if you walk around for a year you get 5 units. If you worked at Sellafield, 50 units a year then they would take you off work for a while to clear you of that. I had 62,000 units. So at some stage, that's going to rear its head up and bite me which is why I have to keep on top of my diet. It's too easy to get back to how I was, so I've given myself a 2-week window where I've eaten shit! It's been wonderful, but tomorrow I go back to a diet and healthy lifestyle.

My particular form of cancer isn't one you can say is caused by x, y or z, it's rare and normally only seen 3 or 4 times a year. There is so little education as we're so indoctrinated. Many people now go for mammograms, which could possibly give you cancer as you're destroying tissue and radiating a very sensitive area so people need to be educated into other ways. You can check with thermal imaging and other kinds of ways. If I was in America and a doctor and had read about certain diets like vitamin B or cannabis oil diet. You come to me and say I have terminal cancer, it's inoperable and radiation won't work. I can't tell you about those other options or I'll be placed into prison due to the strangle hold that the big pharmaceuticals have and it's roughly the same here. $10,000 a month is what we're looking at for treatment.

Royce Gracie says this: *"Self Defence starts with defence against the self"*. So you have to take that degree of self-belief and self-worth into life. We don't have to actually defend ourselves that often, I haven't had to punch anyone for over 10 years, but we have it in us don't we. We're happy to smoke and do drugs and eat shit food though. We as martial arts instructors should therefore be educating people about themselves, before we teach them to punch and kick. I honestly believe that 100%.

Why martial arts Tony?

I started doing Judo as a young kid about 8 or 9 and stuck with it for about 2-3 years. I then did a little bit of Wado-Ryu Karate then dabbled around in my early 20s with various bits and pieces. I was always quite an aggressive person though and my main interest was Rugby. I did a sports teaching course at college, very much on the emphasis on sports coaching so I became quite an adept coach at different things. I wanted to be a professional squash player as I played it semi-pro for a local club in Essex and then I concentrated on my Rugby and got to a fairly good level. I then had quite a bad car accident which nearly broke my neck. I was stationery and a lorry hit me between 50-60 miles an hour and that was it so it curtailed my Rugby career. I then went and enjoyed a very hedonistic lifestyle, big time drug user for years and years, the happy days as I called it. I did some door work up in London and enjoyed it mainly as it was at a fetish club! They were just such good times…! I used to go out Friday night and go to work Tuesday but hadn't been home since! I thought I had to change my life however and moved to Coventry and realised my old days as a sales manager just wasn't me anymore. My hedonistic lifestyle was very addictive for a number of reasons as you can imagine but it had to change and I met Sarah but didn't have a clue what I wanted to do.

I'm a hardworking person but for the first time in my life I thought to myself what am I going to do and nothing fitted. We were really skint but I just thought that there would be something round the corner that would be big. I really believed it and then one day I thought what's this thing on my leg? It was sort of a red swelling on my calf so I went to the doctors who told me I had a DVT probably caused by a sedentary lifestyle as I hadn't done sports for years at this point! I was up to around 19 stone with no fitness! The doctor told me I had to go to hospital but there were no beds so I got an injection to try and hold it in place. I had no idea what it was, but was poking around and dislodged it! My body felt like someone had flushed it, that's the only way I can describe the weird sensation. I'd had what they call a `1 in 3` where it either goes in your brain – stroke, lung – pulmonary embolism, or heart – heart attack and die. I got the one in my lung and hospital for 6 weeks!

I did a lot of soul searching and realised I'd never done anything of any note. I came out of hospital and thought this is life changing time. Then a guy from GKR Karate knocked on the door. I'd never heard of them but I went down there and within 3 weeks I was sparring, knocking the crap out the supposed black belts and then I was approached by the regional manager asking if I wanted a job. So I thought yes this is it! So after around 2 months I took my first class which was an enormous success but as soon as I stood in front of the students, I knew that was my journey. It wasn't a question; I knew that's where I should be. How blessed is that, to find your legend? It all started from there and so within a month I was the highest recruiter in the country and signed up 15-20 people a night, most night's 3 or 4. I had huge classes as I knew how to coach from my College days. My martial arts weren't great but I knew how to teach and that was it! After about 3 months I thought, hang on, this is bollocks what they're teaching, it's all about money! I realised it wasn't for me and went to a big Bob Sullivan seminar, I thought this is wrong so left with every single one of their recruiters and many of their teachers who then followed me. I realised I was doing all the work and so got rid of them and went down to start training with Mo Teague as I wanted the best reality there was.

I used to drive down at 4am to see him and get back at 7pm to go teach. I then just started building up what I was doing and getting the bigger picture. Anyone I saw in *MAI* I was going up to do seminars with and we started getting a good reputation for that. But then me being me said we'll start manufacturing our own mitts, gloves etc. as we wanted to do everything and sometimes lost sight of our way. I then became very friendly with Iain Abernethy. My mum had just got over her first bout of breast cancer and we had no money at all, we were looking down the side of the sofa for change, it was really hand to mouth for 3-4 years where myself and Sarah didn't buy presents or anything. But we had a belief we were on the right path. Then Iain said, if you're ever out in Cyprus, go and see Russell Stutely - I think you'd get on with him. So I booked a two hour private lesson with him when we got out there and got on extremely well with him.

As soon as he started the pressure point stuff I thought this is what I wanted, this is the magic ingredient. The following day I did another 2 hours, the day after that, 3 hours. Sarah said if you go the next day you and I will be divorcing so I did 4 hours that day and the Friday I spent all day with him at his house. I was hooked. I got all his DVDs and got back and practiced. Russ then used me as his Uke when he came over for seminars so I was getting the hang of it and that's where the whole pressure point journey started.

I was naturally good at pressure points and had an innate ability to find them. It was the first thing I was any good at in regards to martial arts. I could fight, but I wouldn't say I was a good martial artist, this was my key. More importantly I realised that if I could teach girls who are 7 or 8 stone where these vulnerable areas were, then that's what I was looking for. So I wanted to put together a system which I felt would work for someone who hasn't got that size or strength advantage. So it all started coming slightly together and I built up a good name fairly quickly. We went over to Peterborough and did a seminar for a jiu-jitsu group. If Russ was being paid, he'd do it and do all the demonstrations on me, if not I'd do it and he said it would be great experience for me. So I did this seminar and there were a lot of very high level Jiu-Jitsu guys there including some 9th Dans. One walks over to me called Joe Carslake and says "You know what; you're the only other fucker here, who could fight fucking sleep! I'd like to show you some stuff". I was then invited to teach a group in Devon on a training weekend, predominantly jiu-jitsu and Joe was there so we had a chat and I started learning from him for around 6 years before we fell out eventually but I got some great information in that time. I headlined SENI and sold out which I think only Bisping and Royce had done that year. It wasn't because I was a particularly big draw, but I worked hard to make sure people knew about it and would come and didn't want to let the organisers down who had given me the opportunity. In that time as well we built a reputation of putting on good events and Sarah has been fantastic at that with the organisation of it all.

We then had opportunities with the school and it started growing more, then I had the opportunity to do a DVD set which went down very well. Where I've scored heavily is where most people don't bother to reach out, I've always been very good at that. For example, I read an article by Richard Bustillo in *Black Belt* magazine and his philosophy echoed mine in that it's about your individual journey. I believe in teaching the individual rather than the mass and that I think is why I've been successful. We have over 400 students now which I never thought was possible! I sit here some nights before I lock up and still picture myself in this place. It's a struggle and it's only this year we've really made any money as we got shafted by the council but I still have to find around £8000 a month before I get a penny. I do it for the love though and because it's what I'm meant to be doing.

Let's talk about the cancer then!

In around the August of 2014 I started getting chest pains, but my physio referred it to a car accident we had had previously in which I damaged my back. When a month or two passed and it was getting worse then a cough came I decided to go and see the doctor. This was in the October and they said maybe as a smoker it's worth getting a chest x-ray. The following day I had the x-ray and the doctors said it would probably be around 8-10 days before I got a result so don't worry if you don't hear anything. 2 days later I go into the office with 3 missed calls from the doctor and at this point I knew something was wrong. That was the worst night in many respects as I was just panicky but I knew. I'd spoken to a friend called Ian Goehler back in the April and knew something was wrong then but I just couldn't pin point it, but felt there was something seriously wrong with me. The doctors said there was something showing up in the x-ray and due to me being a very heavy smoke over the years, I immediately thought lung cancer. But what actually happened was that they saw the mass of the tumour through my lung as it was that big. I then have a nightmare couple of months with Warwick Hospital.

The first meeting I went to for breathing tests etc. - the man turns to me and tells me I have pericardium cancer, no biopsy, no nothing. Pericardium is one of the worst you can get, it's almost bye bye right there. So for a month I'm on a back foot and distraught thinking I'm going to die. It's horrible; there are no words to describe it. They then sent me for a biopsy, 3 times I went over and 3 times they cocked up for various reasons. It was a nightmare. They say if you have lung cancer, go the NHS route as you have a good team around you. I have BUPA however so made an appointment with a guy over here and as it transpires if they'd have done that operation, they would have popped it, it would have spread in days and then game over. So I'm not a religious man, spiritual yes, but I believe somebody was looking after me that day. We worked out there were 7 things that could have gone wrong, and if any of them had happened, I would possibly be dead by now.

I go on the Friday to see my doctor and he says to me I've got cancer, he's going to go in, cut it out then send it off to the lab while I'm still under, I'm booked in for the Monday. That was a good thing as I didn't have time to think or worry about it. He asked me when I wanted it, the morning or afternoon, so I asked when he did his best work?! Did he drink at the weekend?! He said he'd be fine so Monday morning we went in and I didn't realise at that point I had an 8% chance of dying on the operating table. I woke up though thankfully and got out fairly quickly.

It's been a pretty interesting time since then but just before the operation I did the seminar with Mikey Wright and Eddie Quinn as they were the two people I wanted to teach with the most as it could well have been my last seminar, and we're going to do another one this year! The last night I taught here, unbeknownst to me, there had been a Facebook group going round and over 70 people turned up from over the years. I was crying my eyes out and I then realised, with no ego how much I meant to some people. One girl got a train from Sheffield, came, trained, and then got the train back the same night. That was an amazing thing and I'll never forget it.

What nourished me throughout this journey is the love and support I've had from some people, it's been quite exceptional. I've fed off people's good feelings and support. We can do anything we wanted if we wanted to, we could go and get on a plane and just travel. But then when you're diagnosed your world becomes that bed. Facebook and social media gave me that window to look out of with people giving me love and support and that was incredible for me.

Yet through all that, you continued running this successful school, training and teaching on seminars when you could.

On the 28th January 2015 I was given 6 months to live by the doctor. The dojo was struggling and so I was asking about what kind of benefits I could get to keep it going. I would be dead without Sarah's support, they were grim times as you can imagine and I remember going to the MAI awards where I gave a speech. There's a photo from that night with myself and Ian Freeman where I look like Paul Gascoigne's older brother and was just 14 stone. We did the seminar for Jack Bristow and I had a stroke that same day just after.

I almost welcomed having the cancer, which sounds ridiculous, every day it would be in my mind, but I'm 100% glad it happened. If it didn't happen I couldn't tell you what Tony Pillage would be like. The pre-cancer Tony Pillage was a lot less wise. The post-cancer Tony is far more selective in who I spend my time with. I've never taken fools particularly gladly but now I just don't at all. I now know how precious time is. I have my radio show now which was a bi-product of the cancer as they invited me on and liked what I had to say. I've always been into helping people and can now do that on a far bigger scale. I've done the dinners as I always said I'd love to run a proper awards show with amazing people who have been in the martial arts for over 70 years. My circle of friends, of which I have many, all get on with each other individually, I'm not the catalyst so now for example Mikey Wright is working with Kevin Franklin on the Strikemate Product. I feel almost like the spider in the middle of the web which is constantly growing and supporting people

Instead of the politics, the web is a supporting network where people can do stuff together and I think in that respect I've been quite catalystic in that . When people were getting their awards, people shut up and were then talking to each other, not just the people on their tables. We wanted to do something proper for proper martial artists doing a real difference. It was about doing good, not making money. We're got the disabled one happening in October again and I think both have very different energies and purposes, but both are equally as great. We'll start working on that end of May time and it just makes more people push forward and be recognised.

What do you think to the general state of martial arts?

I think there is a divide going on now. I see factions, not styles or association, but factions spreading and I think there is a rising tide of integrity again. People are realising people are in it for the money and the fame, but we're going back to the old ideals of doing stuff for the right reasons. People see a successful club and label it as a McDojo but there is a difference. I gave myself a pay rise this year, £950 a month I take out. This month I gave myself my first ever bonus of £250 and I felt like a king!

We just reinvest in what we do. You have to charge people to give value for what you teach though. I'd give people support for their schools for free and 2 months later I'd get a call and they wouldn't have done anything I had suggested. If you pay for something, you value it and will implement it more than likely. I charge people £50 a week, they get unlimited phone support and either a skype meeting or a meeting here which I prefer. That will usually go for an hour and half or two hours and it worked brilliantly for people and they've all come out of it far, far stronger than they came in - I enjoy doing it and sharing people's success out.

I was walking up the stairs to bed the other night and this thought just came into my head. I've nicked other people's thoughts before, but my thought was that I'm not awfully good at many things apart from being myself, and I'm getting better at that every day. I thought that was quite profound! If you took my martial arts journey, back last year I was made a master under Richard Bustillo…there's only four of us in the UK! It's crazy! How cool is that? Richard Bustillo put me in for the Martial Arts World Hall of Fame! How fucking crazy!

I put my success down to the fact that I work hard when I need to. I'm the laziest bastard I know but everyone has this perception I work hard all the time. I also put my success down to Sarah who sort of sweeps up behind me as I go oh I've got another idea!! Not being funny but Alexander the Great didn't cook clean and wash up, he went and conquered, you need people of different skill sets.

I have an unbelievable belief that stems from the very first GKR lesson that this is where I am supposed to be! A lot of my haters in the early days were quite right! I'm this ex-GKR student like Russ Jarmesty, who all of a sudden has made it to headlining SENI! How did that happen? I have no idea apart from I found pressure points and I'm good at it, and have a belief in helping others. My personality, which I've previously had to curtail, I've now realised that the essence of martial arts for me is being me! If people don't like it, I'm not the right teacher for them but I regularly get 30 people on the mat during the week. We had 55 kids today! Some of the early haters are now starting to come around and take notice however. There are people who weren't big fans of me, now asking me to come and teach on their seminars and so it's gone full circle in many respects. For me it's about having that belief, knowing that I'm doing the right thing for me, for the right reasons and keeping it as honest as I can.

Mick Tully
The Mick Tully show

Mick has a fantastic pedigree in a number of different disciplines from Jeet Kune Do to Combat Submission Wrestling. His hugely popular podcast `The Mick Tully` show has interviewed a number of high quality people, including individuals in this book and has now led to Mick becoming a member of the WOMA team!

Always a great guy he was a pleasure to speak to on his experience in the martial arts and thoughts on life!

Just to set the scene of where we are, we are in a holistic treatment room in Tony Pillage's Dojo, so hopefully all the surfaces are wiped down thoroughly. This is a bit of an odd one for me as normally I'm the one doing this with my podcast Mick's Martial Arts!

Come on then Mick, why did you get into the martial arts?

You're going to like this story; it's actually a really good one! If you've every listened to my critically acclaimed podcast Mick's Martial Arts you might have heard me say this, but this is probably the first time that I'll really talk about it. When I was a kid, I was horrendously beaten by my father and at school. I went over to Ireland with an English accent so got beat up for being English, then I picked up an Irish accent and got beat up over here when I got back! From the first times I can ever remember having memories, I always liked martial arts, I liked Monkey Magic, I was never a Bruce Lee fan but I liked martial arts. I've always liked that it just makes sense. This was back in the days when there was no such thing as an anti-hero; if you were a good guy you did good shit, if you were a bad guy, you did bad shit. I used to read a lot of American comics as well and America just seemed like a really cool place. Now it's just food banks and Donald Trump but back in the day it was unbelievable. The reasons I'm saying all this is that I loved martial arts, but I'd already heard a little bit about Jeet Kune Do from around 13 or 14 years old. It already resonated with me. I always wanted to do martial arts but my father would never take me training so I just immersed myself in this world of comic books. So unless I was the last son of Krypton and was going to be sent back away from Earth, the only people you could really equate to were people like Batman as anyone can be Batman! Alright he's a billionaire and his parents died and stuff, but train enough and you can become Batman! He's a badass and I'd already seen the martial arts and thought you could use that as a way of getting you to the pinnacle of physical condition. I was always interested in martial arts, and I was 15 years of age queuing up to go to an Indie gig in

Coventry. I was that cool kid who was into Morrissey before anyone else and as the joke goes:

Why did the hipster burn his mouth?

Because he drank his coffee before it was cool...

That was me. So I was queuing up to go in and saw Geoff Thompson annihilate these squaddies. It's in his book *Watch My Back*, and immediately once the dust settled I went up to him and asked him what that was. He said Karate so I asked him if he got scared and he replied every day. It was basically like something out of Star Wars where I was like "Teach me Obi-Won"! Let's put it this way, I've never been brave and I've certainly never been hard working. People always tell me I train really hard, I'd love to see what I'd be like if I actually gave a shit. My training now is secondary as I'm hanging out with cool people. But getting back to the training, Geoff said I could go and train with him, but that would have taken two buses when I could get one bus into town and train with a guy called Jim O'Brien. He was a wonderful guy and I was actually one of his pallbearers. Myself and his son were head pallbearers and all 6 of us pallbearers were black belts. He rang me up and said he had leukaemia. I started Karate with him, but he had this awful brown belt who was a real douchebag who used to kick the shit out of me every week. I put up with it for 6 months or so then was like, no that's enough. I respectfully disagree you have to go through the hard stuff in order to get the real training as we're mammals; we want warmth, love and sustenance. So what I did was take the path of least resistance and went to another gym with Andy Margrett who is the guy I got my black belt with. As an aside with Jim O'Brien, when we went in and carried the coffin, we opened it up and all 6 of us were going to put our black belts in and they were going to be cremated with him. I wanted to do that as a symbolic thing where this is actually the point where I don't do Karate anymore. So I turn up with this black belt which has like 17 years of memories in it and I'm like woah! The lads however, had gone and got some others from JD sports for £2 thinking it was more of a symbolic thing. I was like er no, I think he wanted us to throw the actual belts in and he meant that much to me that I did!

Even as a black belt I was still scared of violence however. I got a bit better at giving it out, but I was nowhere near ready for what I thought I was going to get from martial arts. I believe you have a certain amount of shit you have to have in your life. I've now met some seriously famous people and even they've had shit in their life. The first 16 years of my life was like a bad country and western song where the wife dies and even the fucking dog leaves! I had that for the first 16 years, but then that's it, so I feel sorry for you guys who still have a load of shit coming your way. I'm sitting pretty now!! I thought martial arts were the answer to my problems, but it sounds cliché but it just raised a ton of questions, some I'm still trying to answer to this day! So that's how I got into martial arts! A bit of the a-typical story of getting beaten up, hating myself, trying to kill myself twice before the age of 16, just teenage angst to the nth degree. That's what I do now though as I know how wonderful life is now. No one should have a mediocre life. That doesn't mean you will be uber successful, or uber rich, or even uber happy all the time but don't tell me you can't have a dream life because I'm living it. I'm a man of very limited talents really; I'm quite amusing and can spin a yarn quite well. The physical stuff I'm pretty decent at, but I've worked hard at it and in martial arts; the bar is set very low in the UK.

That leads on to our next question for what you think to the standard of martial arts in the UK and abroad!

First of all, surrounding yourself with the right people is of crucial importance as you are the sum total of the five people you spend the most time around. That's not a cliché, it's the fucking truth! If you hang around with pigs you're going to end up dirty. You try and explain that to people, and they argue that they have some mates who are a little douchey, but they're good people. I'm not sure as you'll take on certain characteristics of them in my opinion. As to the level of martial arts, you first have to define what that is. Is it a means to an end? See the reality based guys; their default position is that it's functional and it works. I argue that rohypnol works, but you're not trying to tell me it's good are you? The atomic bomb is functional, but trust me there are a lot of Japanese people thinking it's pretty shit. It depends what you want out of it.

For me, martial arts are a vehicle for personal development, self discovery and being able to see people. When I get my gym, the first sign I'm going to put up is from `Cheers` because guess what, it will be the place where everybody knows your name and are always glad you came. Everyone wants to go to that place. You walk in the door and for two hours a week, or an hour a day you're in an environment where everyone wants to see you and is happy you're there. That right there is a billion dollar industry.

People go to martial arts to defend themselves, but we live in the safest time period ever in history! We've never ever been safer and that's the truth! We don't have wars based on ideology or anything; everything now is based on land grabs. This makes me sound like a conspiracy theorist but we haven't had a war based on anything but money or land for the last 300 years. We don't have to worry about religious or political angst anymore, look at the environment in the

UK. The environment has changed now, it's not like Coventry in the 80's where people were getting pissed up every night and fighting. How are you going to get drunk and get in a fight if the only time you drink is the 8 cans of lager you buy from ASDA on a Saturday night.

We need something for social cohesion as it's the safest time ever, but it's the first time in history we're this interconnected. We are absolutely isolated. We don't know our next door neighbours, but we have 5000 friends on Facebook. Its absolute bullshit and I love Facebook but it's like friendship on your terms. It's fostering a very strange outlook. There's a preamble to this by the way. Facebook is a great way to look at the whole microcosm of the martial arts world. I have friends on there who are nice to me on social media, but would stab me in the back in a heartbeat. I love Tony Pillage but within the first 15 minutes of us having any real conversation I said to him I'm sorry but I don't believe a word of what you teach! But fair play because some people do! So Tony asked me if I thought he was full of shit and I said yes, but so am I so we're now on even ground and level pegging and can be friends!

I think martial arts for what it does for your brain, body and spirit is good. There is no democracy in martial arts, it's like my way or the high way and there's a guy at the top who is all powerful. But then you look at something like Kali where the teacher is at the bottom. I've had people that didn't know their left from right and they're now better than me, I just steer them in the right direction. I don't think we've ever been in a better time for the people who get it to truly appreciate what martial arts can bring to your life and what a joy it is. Having said that I don't think we've ever been in a worse time as we have people punching people in the head if they ask for the time, then claiming that their martial art "works" in real life. You've got all sorts of systems out there like Krav Maga and

Systema. Systema is getting a real hard press at the moment, but it's shit! You've got guys doing death stares and waving their arms around like wacky waving inflatable arm man outside some car dealership. They're throwing their arms around going crazy and you just think what the fuck is that?! I think we're not at the point where we don't need to defend ourselves, but Nike and Adidas sell more sneakers than boxing gloves and people don't fucking get that.

People don't want to be a coward, but fucking run if you can. It's like the hard sparring guys who regularly beat the crap out of each other. One day they'll go mental and kill someone and they'll do a biopsy of their brain and find an abnormality caused by head trauma. I've said this before, MMA is big right now, but it is the herpes of the martial arts world, it'll come back every 2 or 3 years and flair up the weekend you're going to be taking the missus away! People say MMA is huge, but I argue that I come from a generation where Ninjitsu was huge! Where we are in martial arts right now is crazy, it's a good place, but it's a bad place! Fuck that makes me sound vague! Maybe I'm turning into one of those old wise, vague masters!

What style do you see as your main one and why?

I do a few and I'm equally shit at all of them! People train for different reasons, for a lot of people it can be a way of exorcising their demons and I really believe that. What got me into JKD is this. I saw Dan Inosanto as I was never really a fan of Bruce Lee, and here is THE quote for the back of the book from Mick Tully – Jeet Kune Do instructor.

"I've never been scared of a Chinese waiter. So that's why Kung Fu didn't scare me. I've never been scared of a Japanese businessman,

so that's why. I've never been scared by an Israeli. But I've been blown away when I've seen like a 70 year old guy play jiu-jitsu upside down and just be one of the nicest guys in the world"

It wasn't JKD that drew me to JKD, it was Dan Inosanto. I saw him back in the 80's to start with and thought he was awesome. Then found out the Bruce Lee thing and thought it was cool but whatever! I liked the Kali stuff, but it was the whole sensibility behind it. JKD has 27 different arts to it to make the training methodology that we know call Jeet Kune Do! If you train with me Jeet Kune Do is Thai Boxing, Boxing, Wrestling, Weaponry and that's it. I'm a meat and potatoes guy and haven't seen many functional tables that have needed more than four legs.

My training is I see Dan Inosanto once or twice a year, Terry Barnett who I had the pleasure of seeing once or twice a week for 8 years, then Rick Faye from America and Neil Simkin. I have four guys that I'm answerable to as well.

Neil is BJJ but also a Karate world champion, his story is unbelievable and he's the only grown man that I'm scared of! I see him 3 or 4 times a week and he knows where I live! The JKD for me, I like the boxing the BJJ and Thai Boxing but I'm starting to like more and more the Silat and Indonesian arts. There's a lifetime of study in one of those martial arts, and I don't know anyone who has 27 lifetimes. The arts are great as they make you think. People used to say to me you have 27 arts in JKD how can you do them all? So I'd say I'm a builder, a plasterer and can also do carpentry and understand plumbing. I also know the right plumbers to get in for the job. If you're going to be an artist of the martial arts you have a choice. You can be a shit artist; you can be a good artist. You can be one like Van Gogh who wasn't discovered in their lifetime. You can be someone like my hero Michelangelo who wasn't shackled by one art form or discipline, he was unbelievable at all. Da Vinci was successful as he was from bastard birth so was never truly accepted by his father. As a result of that, he wasn't shackled to being an apprentice under this artisan. As no one really wanted him he went to like 4 different art schools. He had a style of his own like JKD. You have a choice and pick the stuff you like and you don't like. Pick the stuff you like and avoid the stuff you don't until you can't avoid it anymore then think that you have to throw everything in to it. The point is that I don't know anyone who's life hasn't been enriched by having more books, or more records, or more of anything. The beauty of Jeet Kune Do is that you get all the top guys just working together. The joke goes:

How many JKD guys does it take to screw in a lightbulb?

No idea as we're still finding 15 different ways of taking it out.

I'm just busy trying to get good so don't want the politics or bullshit. That's why I love Jeet Kune Do. It's a great mindset. I'm not the best martial artist, but I'm a pretty decent teacher.

My anti-bullying program is if someone is on your case, punch them in the throat. There's the argument of oh I'll get into trouble, but you're getting into trouble anyway! The Jeet Kune Do gives me options which give me more chance of success. Average guy in the street is angry, he'll be fucking furious when I break his jaw. People think that because someone is enraged it's like superpower. What is it? Budget X-Men? Just because you're angry you think you're going to frighten me? For me martial arts are an exercise in physical motion. You just have to reframe your thoughts. It's heavy but that's what life is all about. It's a cool journey and you get to hang out with cool people!

Let's plug your show Mick's Martial Arts then! Tell us about it!

The show started because of Anthony McGinley who is a great friend of mine and the technical wizard behind what we're doing with Technical Headphones. He's done it all; he was at the BBC, producer for the Chris Moyles show and with Chris Evans. He was at Capital Radio for a while, then got a gig at Virgin Megastore on Oxford Street and would basically sit there and just talk shit all day. He was like the in-house DJ but it was great as he was in Oxford Street getting paid a ton! Then he came up to Coventry and Warwickshire and started working with Mercia Sound. He had the hottest rated breakfast show in the UK with a friend of mine, Helen Knott, and they had this real madcap early morning show which was great.

I said if they were ever having a slow day, ring me up and ask me something and I'll give an opinion on it! I just say anything that will just upset people! They had this quiz called `May the Fourth be with you` which shockingly had a theme to it! So he rang me up and said 10 questions in a minute on Star Wars! I got to the 9th question and the 10th was `Who played Anakin Skywalker in *Attack of the Clones*. So instead of saying Hayden Christensen I said, like a dweeb as I knew it, Jake Lloyd and the buzzer went and I just went "FUCK" on live radio. After that, we just hung out!

I then met Matt Hocker who was announcing and we started chatting. He'd done a bit of bouncing and a little martial arts and we started training. I tell you what if you want to learn Shakespearean level treachery, get into radio as its brutal! You can be on air, and then finish a show thinking everything is okay. Then you'll come out and they'll be like, you have 15 minutes to clean your desk get out! Matt went through a bit of a hard time and just wanted to train and needed to hit stuff! But I was like no I won't let you hit stuff and externalise your rage, you need to be integrated into society through wrestling as my ball-bag will be two inches away from your face while we do that, you can't get more integrated. So we started wrestling and he started doing privates with me for free. We just trained and enjoyed and figured some shit out. Then next thing you know he gets a job with P&O, then Disney, then he's head of entertainment all around the Caribbean. He's gone from being at the bottom to being right at the top and meeting his fiancée. He said, I wouldn't have done any of that if it wasn't for you. He was talking like he was saying goodbye before this so that's how we got into it.

He was then in the car with me one day and heard me and Rick Faye talking and was like, shit if we record this and put it out on a podcast it will be amazing. I only just know what an MP3 is, I don't get it! I was never going to be a Netflix guy I'm always a box set guy. Its technology I can't get my head around. He told me what a podcast was and said you're the most famous, charismatic un-famous person I know! I've created myself this way in fairness. The Mick Tully I am wasn't meant to be like I am! So that's how we did it and started the podcast.

The first few I just basically enrolled friends of mine, but I'm lucky as a lot of my friends were also my heroes so it was cool! It was going great so I thought people will get to know who I am, listen to my humour and I'll get a few seminars out of it with my mercenary head on. I didn't think it would get this big however! I then met Will Henshaw of *Mind, Body and Kick-Ass Moves* and said 'So you did *Mind, Body and Kick-ass Moves* with Chris Crudelli?' and he just snarled at the mention of Crudelli. So I said, if he'd got someone charismatic, funny, unconventionally handsome like me, he would have been on series 10 right now and we'd be doing something like *An Idiot Abroaa.* I said let's do something and the following week he asked me to go and interview Van Damme with him which is a whole other story! JCVD is something else! The guy is a maniac! We did find out we worked really well together though and it was just really, really cool! We interviewed some cool people, some famous, some other not so famous. We then started filming others like Eric Paulson, Bob Breen, and Francis Fong etc! Bellator we did as well for some filming and while we were down there I was sat next to Joe Long from Fighters Inc. I walk in and we're eating quails eggs and caviar as they'd asked us to be there. Chance meetings led to all this!

I live a pretty dream life and people always say follow your dreams! Most of us don't have bad lives through. If you have a roof over your head, can read and write and live in the developed world, you'll be okay. You've won the karmic lottery. I had no idea any of this was going to happen but I'm a chancer and I'm now being paid to talk shite. I'm shocked it took the world 47 years to work out what I knew when I was 16!

It's tricky to be in this game full time if you want to sleep at night. It's when you start getting into these contracts that people can't get out of then it gets into a very grey area. For me I get paid, but I'm also a friend, mentor etc. I don't like the direct billing thing where you're tied in for 36 months or whatever. I have a friend who is a great guy and is very successful, but he says fuck them. If they sign and get tied in to 36 months that's their fault, you don't see people taking their sofas back to DFS then crying after. From a business point of view he has a valid point; we all have bills to pay. But for me when you shackle someone in to a credit agreement, you're the Josef Fritzl of martial arts! The students stay with you because they have to! It wasn't a negotiation. I think you should be able to opt out. I have guys who train with me and I won't charge them as right then it's not a good time for them financially. But then others, I'm like 'sorry you have to pay.' I have two students who pay me £60 an hour.

I don't want anyone in my life that doesn't bring me joy; you don't need it unless you're stuck in a job. But I don't think anyone is that stuck in a job. You can always change your life if you want to. The more and more you look at martial arts, the more and more you realise that we need people in the world who can kick another person's arse. The only way to deal with violent people is through good men skilled at it. As martial artists and teachers our role is to turn around and go you know what, you need a bit of fucking monster put into you. Better more functional people for a better more functional world! For the martial artists reading this don't ever think there is an end to the journey, it's a conveyor belt. It just goes in a circle and circuit and never ever stops. Some people jump on, some jump off. But while you're on it, subliminally you're having a bit of monster beat into you through the drills.

Stewart McGill
Urban Krav Maga

Stewart McGill is a Chief Instructor of Urban Krav Maga. He's been teaching Krav in some form or another full time since 2003 and before this he was 3rd Dan in Goju Ryu Karate. He first began training in 1972 with Judo and has done various things since then including Boxing and Muay Thai as well as Goju Ryu.

Where did it all begin for you then? Do you remember walking in to your first class and what got you started?

I started with Judo in 1972 and like most people was a bit intimidated, but really enjoyed it and did it for a few years. I didn't particularly train very regularly, and wasn't very interested in the whole going for the belts gig. I'm not a big fan of chasing the belts as we'll probably discuss later. The first class I remember pretty well and it was tough, there were people there younger and smaller than me knocking me about; we still attempt to make Leverage a big feature of what we teach.

How long did you do Judo for then and then when did you decide to pursue other avenues?

It was around 3 or 4 years that I stuck with Judo then took 2 or 3 years off and just did a bit of boxing and Muay Thai. I played around for quite a large part of the 80s just doing various things here and there and going from club to club; it wasn't really until the late 80s early 90s when I really settled down to do Goju Ryu Karate.

I was working in the City of London, I apologise to everybody but to afford a house in London in those days that's where you had to work. Just up the road from my office was Chris Rowen who was a very prominent teacher of Goju Ryu karate. So I went up there and trained with him. It was mostly stand up, Chris had a Ju-jitsu black belt but he was very much for teaching a traditional Goju Ryu syllabus which tried to avoid going to the ground. To a certain extent I appreciate the philosophy of "don't go to the ground" but it just isn't always possible.

This was in the late 80s before the UFC's rise to prominence. Broadly speaking, in the 80s you had to worry about Ninjitsu and Taekwondo people trying to kick you in the head, as the 90s developed you had to deal with people wanting to take you down and break something or get your back and choke you. Even though most people still wanted to give you a right hander, I felt it increasingly necessary to develop some ground-fighting skills.

When were you first introduced to Krav Maga then?

I think I first saw something about Krav Maga in the late 90s, it was a Krav Maga Induction Course covered in a magazine. The course lasted Friday evening, and all day on Saturday and Sunday. I wasn't wholly convinced by all the techniques but I liked the style of training, which was basically "this is the problem, what's the solution?"

Though not convinced by all the stuff they taught, I did like the fact they had a ground game designed from a self defence viewpoint, even if it wasn't particularly developed and contained some pretty big mistakes.

The late 90s was quite a busy time for me as we had our first kid in 1997 and my second in 1999, so I was basically just training at a few clubs here and there. I tried Kempo Jiu-Jitsu for a while and a bit of boxing. But I found as I got into my late 30s and early 40s, no matter how fit you keep yourself, you get hit more often. My wife was not too happy when I came back with a bloody nose or black eye after sparring with guys half my age. First few rounds were fine but anybody who tells you that age is just a number hasn't really put that theory to a proper test, the puff goes a little no matter how much you keep yourself in trim.

This is when I thought "I'm probably going to have to knock this on the head." I was also having issues with my job at this point and the opportunity came up to do the Krav Maga Instructor course in 2003. That kind of worked out nicely as it was just about that time I lost my job in the city. I wasn't too unhappy about that as I hated it and it gave me the kick in the ass I needed to go ahead and teach martial arts full time. And it's moved on nicely from there.

What do you think of the state of martial arts today then? Do you separate martial arts and self defence and which one do you class Krav Maga as?

I don't like all this bullshit of "it's not a martial art it's a self defence system:" it's a martial art. Different martial arts have different focuses or emphases but they all have a martial intent and you have to study them like mastering an art. I think a lot of people want to disassociate Krav Maga and other systems from the martial arts heading because they associate the latter with flowery "irrelevant" stuff like kata.

I can relate a lot of the things we do back to kata. A lot of kata is actually misunderstood and some of the applications taught are poor, which I think aggravates its bad reputation amongst many.

People like to separate things and say "this is stand up, this is ground, this is reality fighting and this is martial arts". To me it's all related and the best Reality practitioners have solid bases in the traditional martial arts: concepts such as "position then technique" can't just be forgotten because "in my style there are no rules"

I think there is certainly an element of "McDojo" in the Krav Maga world and martial arts in general. Now there is nothing wrong with running things on a business-like basis; however; there are certain people who are maybe a little too focussed on the commercial side and I can see why some people criticise that. We try and keep it going on a commercial basis but at the same time don't want to lose the joy and the art of just doing the stuff, and we don't push merchandise and t-shirts big time.

This thing about the McDojo is nothing new. In the old days, whenever It was Christmas it was often time to do a grading and pay for Sensei's Christmas presents or whatever, it has been around for a lot longer than people really realise. McDojo is just a new word.

I think martial arts today are in quite a good place, people will always say things were better 30/40 years ago, about anything. There's more variety out there and there are more people doing martial arts which are more immediately practical. If you did say Goju Ryu Karate or Judo you'd probably be able to handle yourself across quite a lot of situations but it would take a long time. And you don't really have specific weapons defences; though I do believe that these are lost in the Kata. Sometimes when we've been developing stuff or analysing what we do I get a wee epiphany that takes me back to a Kata move.

There are so many more direct systems around now where you can learn something quick and that's ultimately a good thing, though everything they do should be informed by good martial arts principles. I remember people coming to us in the Goju Ryu days wanting to learn how to defend themselves and wondering why they were doing Kata. As you go into the reality based systems more deeply you realise a large part of what you're doing is about getting feet and hips in the right place, achieving appropriate stability and making a transition from one stance to another. Then you realise a hell of a lot of it is in the Kata , took me around 30-40 years to properly get that. People now want to learn things a little more quickly which is fair enough and there are more opportunities to do so. An issue I have is some of the reality based instructors clearly don't have a background in traditional martial arts and that really undermines the quality of their teaching.

There are also a lot of good places to learn the ground game these days, the growth of BJJ in particular has been good for the state of

British martial arts and made many teachers realise that you need to be able to teach a proper ground game, even if it's only to counter Ju Jitsu.

How important do you think it is for instructors teaching reality to have real life experience of violence?

I think it's good to have that background and to be able to call on some of those experiences. I tend to use those experiences as examples of what not to do, things to avoid. For example, I once took a shot at a guy in the ribcage. I had a pretty good traditional karate stance and a lot of anger so it was a pretty good strike I have to say. As I hit him, I could feel he had a book in his pocket that took the blow and the next thing I see is a big right hand coming over which put me on the floor! So from that I learnt that if its winter in Scotland and the guy has a big coat on...don't go for the body shots!

The people we have in our system are a mixture of people who have real life experience and those that haven't. Someone who hasn't had much of that experience can still be a great teacher and if they've learnt from someone who has and have the ability to impart that knowledge effectively. There also isn't anything wrong with doing martial arts for the art side, if you like the kata and tradition it will still be of benefit to you in terms of conveying fundamental concepts of positioning and technique. As you may have noticed, the concept of position then technique is very important to me and I would rather have someone teaching who understood that concept and could explain it, than someone who had been in hundreds of real life fights but couldn't communicate. On that last point, there are plenty of people that can handle themselves very well, but can't teach to save their lives, which I guess is the converse of your question.

The belt system is a staple of martial arts, what are your issues with it?

It's always been an issue for me when people train for the belt. You train to get a black belt, so you can say you're a black belt then stop. For me you train to get better, not go through a particular syllabus or get a belt. We have a grading system and it gives me a structure to teach and one thing I want to do this year is focus more on getting people the grades.

But a lot of people just want to turn up and train and what really counts is how you handle yourself on the pressure tests that we do on a regular basis. If you reach a high rank, there's also a slight belief that you're better than other people and so some distancing happens between senior and non-senior grades, which I really do not like.

There are always people better than others, but when I've been to some other clubs over the years, even before the class begins people separate into groups of belt colour with the white belts being ignored and the beginners just left wondering what to do. I will always think that kind of sucks.

Part of the appeal of Krav Maga in its early day in the UK was "no uniforms and no grading that you need to shell out money for" That certainly seems to have changed.

Going back slightly to the pressure testing then, how important do you think that is?

You have to be able to handle yourself and do it under pressure. If you've trained a bit, are working with people you're comfortable with, there's no verbal aggression, and you're in pretty good condition, handling challenges in a dojo can be relatively simple.

You can never replicate the stress of a real situation in a dojo, but you can try to get as close as you possibly can. I always tell people to give it some if they're attacking and give some verbal aggression too, so we get people screaming obscenities at each other. I like people doing some vigorous exercise before being put into a pressure situation so you start from a stressed, disadvantageous position. For example, we get them to beat the shit out of a bag for a minute, then put them in a situation after jumping up and spinning 5 times to make you dizzy. That can be a little intimidating for some and it makes the initial attacks a tad tough to handle.

It's a good thing to replicate the shock factor and a shadow of the stress that you'll be under in a real situation so for me pressure testing is important, but so is safety so you have to manage it carefully.

What do you think makes a good instructor then? Is there a way you structure your classes?
To be a good instructor you have to be a good listener and a good observer of watching what people do. You have to realise that as an instructor it isn't about you, it's about the students and what they need.

I've seen people make it all about them and what they want to teach, not what the students need.

You have to listen to what people say. I had some girls last night who were quite critical about a technique I was showing and I asked them to repeat it a few times. They had misunderstood the technique slightly and I could then see where the criticism arose from. I then explained how it needed to be done and they got it great, but I didn't take offense to the criticism. I listened. I think you also need to realise as an instructor that people are different and the best technique for someone is the one that works best for them. You can't expect Big Mike who's 6ft 4 and 21 stone to do the same technique as a 5ft 2, 7 stone girl with the same effect, so you need to be able to tailor the training.

If someone isn't getting something, you can't just tell them to try harder; you need to explain better as it's primarily your fault. So there are many personal qualities you need as an instructor as well as your actual ability to do the stuff and impart knowledge.

The way I structure is pretty standard. We do a short warm up as don't want to waste too much time, then some techniques as a group mixing the senior and newer people. We then do a little pressure test, then separate the class with the seniors and new ones.

Then I try to relate the last techniques we covered to the first set so people can see the connection: the plethora of techniques in a comprehensive system like ours can be daunting so I try to get people to understand early on that everything derives from a basic kernel of knowledge and movements.

What are your plans for the future then?

I always want to reach more people and teach more people. I believe very firmly in what we do and the principles we teach. I think we are a pretty good fusion of the traditional and modern martial arts. We have some very experienced traditional martial artists with us including the great Leo Negao, former world BJJ champion, so we can really look at things in depth, which I think is a great thing!

I want to see more people doing it, not just from a commercial view, but because I think we do good stuff. We'll probably do a lot more in terms of online courses, the first one of which we've released already on Udemy, defending the 10 most common attacks.

We can produce that and interact with people who might not be able to handle the pressure of a dojo situation and maybe what they learn can enhance their confidence and give them a chance if it kicks off.

How important do you think the internet is in terms of martial arts then?

I think it's a great thing for people to be able to put stuff out there and spread the knowledge. Now it's very easy to comment on a video and just say, "this is crap." If you're sensitive, don't publicise your training videos, no matter how good you are! There will always be those people who just bitch and say it's shit.

I sometimes ask those people, if you don't think it will work, tell me why and show me an alternative. That's how I think people should handle it; I've yet to have anybody respond with an alternative that wasn't total nonsense to be honest.

The internet can reflect the appetite for the sensational, but that's not the fault of the net in itself, people just like the sexy stuff. I don't teach a lot of gun threat techniques but those videos get a lot of interest! Unless you're in the drugs business it's pretty unlikely a gun will be pulled on you, but we always get a lot of views and responses to anything involving a gun, much more so than those covering more likely scenarios such as someone taking a swing at you.

Having said that, we have had 3 people over the last 4-5 years had guns pulled on them and walked away so it can happen. Some say you will always freeze if a gun is pulled on you, this actually isn't always the case and there is footage out there of people not freezing and taking the weapon; I sent that footage back to some doubters to demonstrate their errors. That's a good thing about the internet; you can share information much easier and adduce information to gainsay some of those people who delight in saying "it's all bollocks" and perpetuating other facile misconceptions.

People will still always want to train in a real place and real environment, so I don't think the net will cause any decline in clubs or academies, though it does provide one more reason to stay at home.

I think everyone should try a few martial arts and do a bit of ground, bit of stand up, bit of reality etc. I think it's very true when people say it's 50% the style and 50% the teacher so it's always good to shop around a little bit and social media allows people to see what is available and compare teaching styles as well as techniques.

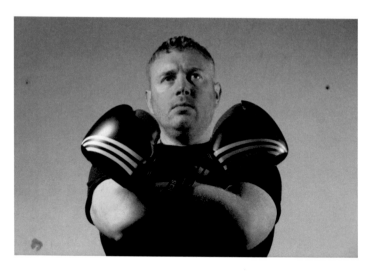

Dean Williams

PKA Kickboxing

Dean has been teaching martial arts for over 20 years now and has experience in Kickboxing, Boxing, Karate and Gracie Jiu-Jitsu. In 2003 he got into the film industry and has now appeared in over 50 productions his most recent being `Enter the Cage`. A national champion, Dean now teaches regularly as well as still being heavily involved in film work and producing.

When did you begin your journey in the martial arts Dean?

I began martial arts in the mid 80's with Toru Takamizawa at the then famous Temple Martial Arts in Birmingham. Here I also trained with Eugene Codrington. After a few years of Wado Ryu karate, I had a few years off before dabbling with a bit of boxing before starting kickboxing. I took to this art as I was a good kicker and not too bad with my hands and loved the many techniques and all over body workout it provided. I also liked how we would train technical work with points fighting, light continuous and full contact as well as street combat applications as well. The club I joined was the PKA which were the founders of kickboxing back in 1974 when both Bill `Superfoot` Wallace and Joe Lewis became world champions. I had many occasions to train with these legends and call them friends.

My biggest influence was my main instructor - the late Mark Shore , he was such an under-rated fighter; big, strong, fast and a character. I remember watching him at the 1997 World Championships with the likes of Nathan `Megatron` Lewis and Faisal Mohammed. Mark was son of the great Lau Gar instructor George Shore.

I got my PKA black belt late 90's and have been teaching that style for 20 years now. In 1999 I won a British middleweight kickboxing title to complement my many national titles and in 2003 I captained an England team where we fought in Austria.

Also in 2003 I got asked to be in a martial arts movie, I'd always wanted to get into TV/film and stunt work but was pretty focused on building my business up. Then after that little job I got a few job offers here and there as my name got out there, and now I have over 50 feature films to my name. It's been a long slog to pursue that career alongside teaching and transferring from doing moves that look good on the big screen to the next day doing moves that are street effective.

Rather than scale down my own training as more movie work came up I saw this as a great opportunity to learn some extra skills such as weaponry, tricking, capoeira and ju-jitsu amongst many styles I've dabbled in, as knowledge is power and not all directors want to see a fancy Hong Kong style fight - most want a realistic bar room brawl or an efficiently trained assassin.

What are your thoughts on the current state of martial arts in the UK?

My thoughts on the current UK martial arts scene are mixed - like any trade, whether a builder, mechanic, estate agent or martial arts instructor, there are good and bad. It's not for me to judge, I just get my head down and teach and do what I do best. If you're good at your job you get plenty of recommendations - if you're not, you soon get found out.

Because I teach such a multitude of techniques and styles within my multi style system I sometimes teach ring fighting, fitness, technique, pad-work, drills for strength, speed, flexibility, I also teach forms as well as the flashy stuff. But always explain the stuff that works and what doesn't, they kind of work that out for themselves.

Can you tell us of any real life altercations you've had?

It's been a long time since I've been in an altercation as I'm normally good at diffusing situations, using confidence and a strong posture rather than a weak position to let them know I'm not one to be pushed around. I remember one incident I calmed down and I'm very good at being vigilant when I'm out as I don't drink and always have my back to the wall. But about 10 minutes after the incident I calmed down which was between a friend of mine and another guy, this guy about 6 foot 3 (I'm 5 foot 6) came back and blindsided me and smashed a bottle over my head. I just automatically went into the zone and pretty much before the shattered glass had hit the floor I'd hit him a few times, I hit him with about 10 -15 clean punches, the 2nd or 3rd one had knocked him out and the others either kept him up or I just drilled him before he went down. In fact he ended up in the ladies toilet as we covered about 6 meters in a straight line through the door of the toilet until he hit the wall in there. Then I noticed my forehead was bleeding from the bottle, I went and got medical attention while they stretchered him out. I got the sympathy as it was self defence but I did worry a little about being done as apparently his face was in a mess. Apparently the doormen were passing the footage around as it was pretty cool and then all of a sudden it disappeared which was a relief! News got round my hands were devastating, felt like saying you should see my kicks then!

What can the martial arts bring to people's lives?

I think martial arts are an amazing pastime, lifestyle, and exercise. I've seen the benefits first hand with children, adults and special needs getting so much out of it. From self preservation, health benefits, mentally, physically and socially and it had opened up so many avenues for me, working with people like Steven Seagal, Jean Claude van Damme and Benedict Cumberbatch.

What are your plans for the future?

Hopefully the future will see me grow my schools a bit more I'm currently bringing some instructors through as I want to keep giving to my students who have been so loyal over the years and I want to carry on learning. I've had the pleasure to train with the likes of Royce, Carley and Renzo Gracie as well as Erik Paulson. I'd also like to carry on working on some cool films both as an actor/stunt performer as well as fight/stunt coordinator and producer.

 Big thanks to my friends Dan and Lucci for putting this together , if anyone would like to hear about my various schools and career then follow me on Twitter @deancrazylegs

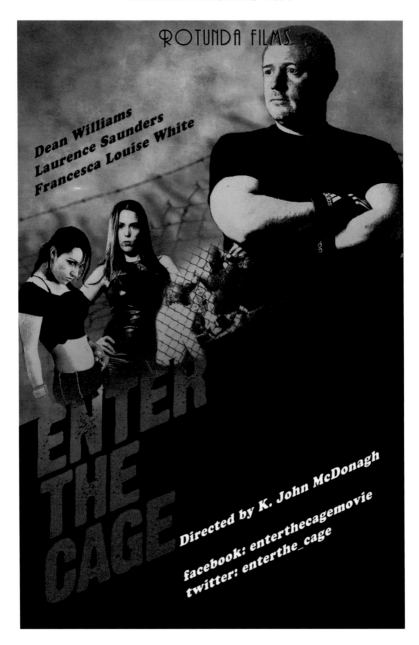

Matthew Chapman

Mittmaster/Masters Academy

Matt started training in martial arts when he was 10 years old and now holds numerous black belts in different disciplines, as well as a British MMA Title. He has now developed his own series of pad drills called Mittmaster which are being used by martial arts schools around the country and abroad.

In addition to this, Matt also runs his own business workshops for martial artists looking to improve their student numbers or grow their school. A published author, Matt is always a great guy to talk to with a wealth of experience in the martial arts.

So you started at a pretty early age of 10 with Ninjutsu. Can you remember what it was like walking into your first class? How did you feel?

Yeah I was super excited as I thought I was going to be a ninja and learn some awesome stuff – climb and fly, use swords etc. And you kind of do apart from the flying bit! There are 24 levels of training in Ninjutsu and some very random techniques like using a blow pipe. When you're 10, believe me, learning how to use a blowpipe is amazing! We got to learn how to throw knives, disarm swords, horse riding, and escape and evasion stuff, it was amazing fun! I loved it, it was great. I turned up for the first class super excited and absolutely loved it immediately so stuck with it and got my first dan black belt from Dusty Miller.

You then moved onto the Filipino martial arts? What made you shift focus slightly?

My instructor Dusty moved to Canada and I was training with the other black belts and it just wasn't quite the same. And I was also having a few issues with the functionality of Ninjutsu. I sparred with a brown belt in Karate and he just punched and kicked holes in me and I was a bit like "Oh, damn" so I went on a bit of quest to find something a little more functional. Some of the Ninjutsu techniques for me, didn't work that well, so I started to open my mind a little. I read things like *The Tao of Jeet Kune Do* by Bruce Lee and realised there was a lot more out there!

How important do you think functionality is for the martial arts? Obviously people study arts for different reasons, some compete, some self-defence, some health.

I think you need to be able to defend yourself first. You should be able to effectively defend yourself against a single attacker and neutralise the threat. There is something very, very wrong with your training if you can't defend yourself against an untrained attack. However, when you start adding in multiple people, or weapons, it's very difficult to `win`; it's more about surviving at that point. I'm pretty confident that if you put most people in front of me, one on one, unless they're equally trained in martial arts they will go down. So yeah, I think it's very important, you need to have that confidence and belief in yourself that you can defend yourself and your loved ones if you need to.

After that, it's almost limiting to just focus purely on self-defence. The tool set for a self-defence situation is very small. If you want to develop as a martial artist you need to look wider and broader and start learning from other martial arts and systems. This is where you go more into the 'arts' side of training. You become better-rounded as a martial artist once you get past doing self-defence only. I also don't want to be training functional self-defence all day every day for 50/60 years. You want to maintain your functional skills of course, but if you want to develop to your potential you need to study other martial arts deeply.

In terms of the sports side of martial arts then, can you remember your first fight? Walking out for the first time to compete?

There were no cages at that time, can you believe it? Only the UFC had the cage or octagon, all the UK MMA fights at that point were in boxing rings, so that's how long I've been around! I remember walking in and feeling pretty relaxed, I'm quite a low stress, calm person so I wasn't actually that nervous. I'd been training martial arts for 15+ years at this point so I knew I could kick and punch, and my grappling at the time was probably one of the best in the UK as I'd been doing it longer than most. We started grappling when the first BJJ instructor came over to the UK, a guy called

Chen. We were one of his first students so we'd been doing it a long time. Plus, we were training with Erik Paulson who was ahead of everyone in the field then, so I wasn't particularly nervous.

I don't get particularly nervous about fighting. In a sporting context it's actually quite safe, it's not like street where someone can stick a knife in you and you're dead. In the cage you might get beaten up a bit, or you'll get tapped out. If you're getting hit too much and you fall down in a foetal position the ref will stop it. And if you get knocked out you're not going to know anything about it anyway! So it didn't really scare me, which is weird! I think most people are intimidated by it but if you think logically you're not really going to get that badly hurt. You might get hurt a bit for a few days or lose in front of your friends but everyone recovers from a fight within a week or two.

I think it was Geoff Thompson who told me about dogs and vacuum cleaners. Dogs can be massive and ferocious but are absolutely terrified of vacuum cleaners even though they could rip one to bits in a matter of seconds. The reason dogs are scared of vacuum cleaners is that they don't understand what they are. A lack of understanding creates fear. I think a lot of people also don't understand what competitive martial arts are about and blow it up in their mind too much. It's really not that scary. If you have good skills, are fit and well-conditioned fighting in a ring or cage is not that scary in my opinion! Other people find it terrifying though! I have friends who are sick before fights and have such bad nerves they can hardly function; they'll doubt themselves and get in a negative mind-set. I never really had that.

The only fighter I ever fought who I was a bit wary of was a guy called Amir Subasic who's a Muay Thai coach in Luton. I read his bio about his life, he was in the military and he's a tough guy, with a lot of experience! He'd knocked out many people before and I thought "I really need to take this guy down quick or he will knock me out!" Luckily for me I did! But if I hadn't taken him down he would have knocked me out for sure! So he was the only opponent who had me worried, and even then I didn't get too worked up.

After that I popped one of the ligaments in my knee whilst grappling so that was end of my fighting career, as it would go every time I tried to prepare for a fight. But I wasn't really fighting for the glory or for the money or anything like that. I just fought because I wanted to test myself and see how good my skills were. Once I got injured there didn't seem to be much point in continuing to fight. If you just fight to test yourself, eventually you'll meet someone who is a real fighter and just loves to fight, and you're going to lose. So I kind of realised that it was time to quit!

At what point did you think you wanted to teach full time and make a career out of martial arts?

I started teaching quite early on really, I think I was brown belt in Ninjutsu and helped out in classes. I just enjoyed helping people out and sharing my knowledge. That continued once I started with JKD and I then opened up a kickboxing club at my University. I've been teaching probably since I was 16 years old.

I find teaching so much more rewarding than fighting. I would fight and even if I won conclusively it was a bit anti-climactic. I didn't get a massive rush and run round the cage screaming like you sometimes see people do. I'd be like, "yeah, cool I won", then I'd go and have a beer. I find teaching way more enjoyable and love seeing people improve and overcome hurdles and get better. I like teaching kids that get their junior black belts then keep training and earn adult black belts, who then start instructing or fighting and win titles of their own. That's so much fun for me! That's way more satisfying for me than punching people in the face!

You now run the Master's Academy in Essex. When did you decide to make the jump to go full time with martial arts?

I was at university and we were getting to the end of the degree in Sports Science and I suddenly thought "Oh shit we need to make some money now". I realised I needed to get a job, but I'm basically unemployable as I don't take direction well and think I'm smarter than most bosses! I'd be a nightmare employee so I literally didn't have any choice it was make it work or starve. I had to do what I love to make money!

We lived in a very poor area of East London called Barking at that point and we thought about opening up there. But I quickly realised that it would be very difficult to make a living there as people didn't have any money. So we got in our car and drove round and came to a place in Essex called Loughton and it was totally different! Massive houses, Bentleys and Porches everywhere and we both went, "Yep, let's set up a business here". It just made more sense to build a business in an affluent area. We rented a space at a David Lloyd club and set up a class there which got very busy very quickly. Then 2 years later we moved into a full time place and we've been there ever since, which is pretty cool!

What do you think are the most important elements to being a good martial arts instructor?

Well you need students to be a teacher first of all! Whether people want to learn from you long term can be partly due to your expertise or reputation, but ultimately it's to do with how likeable you are. You have to be a nice, likeable person to keep students for the long haul. I've been taught by some instructors who are technically amazing but they're not very likeable and don't have many students as a result of that. To be successful you've got to be a good person who has their student's interests at heart. Unfortunately in martial arts there are quite a few weirdos and strange personalities!

Also make sure you have drilled the material you want to teach till the point where you can't do it wrong. Sometimes people start teaching a bit early and their technique isn't quite there and they're still making mistakes. You need to drill techniques into your nervous system to a point where you can't do it wrong.

Then you need to have a basic understanding of how to teach. Frequently in martial arts, fighters don't make the best teachers because they can physically do 'stuff' but they can't break it down well enough to teach. So a basic understanding of how to teach and motivate people is really important.

Then there's the passion for sharing your knowledge with people. Passion is what keeps you going when you have problems in your school and things aren't going well. You need to have a burning passion for martial arts as passion is infectious. If you meet an instructor who is really passionate about what they teach, they draw you in and that's rare nowadays. People doing jobs they hate tend to not have much passion in their lives. But when you meet someone truly passionate who loves something with their entire being, it's very attractive and you'll attract people who share that vision.

As well as teaching now, you are also a published author, run business seminars for martial artists and have created the Mittmaster system. When was the point when you thought, right I'm going to do something a bit more than just teach?

I've always been quite good at English (I'm sure my English teacher would disagree) and just thought that it would be pretty cool to be an author. Part of me just wanted to be an author and do something different, but also I just wanted to get my message out to more people. So I just started writing stuff and my first book was about pad drills because I love pad training. All experienced martial artists are excellent at one thing, and my thing is pad drills. I'm great at creating them, designing them and training them. So my first book was about pad drills and I just wanted to share it with people.

That book is available free if you go to my website, www.mittmaster.com. Also when we went to MMA shows people didn't know how to train properly to win their first MMA fight. We were cleaning up. Our win rate at our school at the moment is around 90%, meaning if we put 10 fighters in to fight, 9 will win, which is very high. Other schools just didn't know how to train their fighters to win.

So I wrote a book about that as I just wanted to help people out and that sold quite well. It was called *How to win your first MMA fight* and it was literally just that – the strategy to win if you don't really know what you're doing.

I then wanted to write about martial arts business as I've met a lot of incredibly talented martial artists who have no idea how to run a profitable school. This is because you don't get taught that by your instructor, you just get taught how to kick and punch. Then you go and open a class and you start your own school. That's not necessarily the best way to start a business however. I've done a lot of training on business and spent a lot of my own money getting educated. I've also made every mistake you could possibly make from the word go, so I've got a pretty good grasp of martial arts business at a basic level.

Martial artists are weird, really we should get business training from business professionals but martial artists would much rather get business training from another martial artist. I wanted to write a book about martial arts business to help people out. There are so many good instructors out there who are struggling. They're elite martial artist's but have a class of 10 and can't keep people long term. So I wrote my book *Black Belt Biz* to help them to run a successful business.

Being a school owner is a great job to have. There is so much freedom if you set it up right, it's a fantastic way of life because you can get up when you want, do some training, teach some classes then go home and relax! You get to share your passion with a lot of free time and flexibility. The earning potential is very good if you know how to market yourself and run a business effectively. It's possible to make a pretty comfortable living doing it.

There is also a big thing in martial arts with old school instructors being anti making money. I find the best martial arts instructors are the ones who can only purely focus on martial arts. If you have to have a day job and then have to go and teach it's good but it doesn't leave much free time or energy for your own research or training or to go to seminars and hang out with other martial artists.

I find the best instructors in terms of skill are the "professional ones" who spent time training and learning. In order to do that you can't have a regular job. You either need a trust fund or a way of funding that lifestyle so it makes sense to charge appropriately for your lessons. That way you have extra income to spend on your own training and development, which ultimately benefits your students. It's a ridiculous argument to say there should be no money in martial arts.

MittMaster.com is now what you're predominantly known for. When did you decide to do it and package it and take it out?

I read a lot about business and one of the main rules for financial stability is to have passive income. This means you earn money even when you're not working. The problem with martial arts classes is that you have to go and teach them. Ha ha. If you cancel them, you don't earn, if you're injured, you don't earn, if you're ill, you don't earn. It's financially risky to just have all your eggs in one basket.

I needed a source of passive income that allowed me to earn money when I wasn't teaching classes. So I researched and spent loads of money on internet marketing training. Part of that training is creating products you can sell. The advantage of selling videos that are downloadable is that I don't have any stock, someone buys a video and they get sent a link and I make a small profit minus the transaction cost.

So I was thinking, what could I offer the world that I'm passionate about? I'm an okay grappler, but not great. I'm not really a fighter, there are plenty of better fighters than me, but in my humble opinion, I have the best pad training system in the world. I've seen fantastic pad trainers in boxers, and Muay Thai for example but I haven't seen anyone who can put it together like I have over 5-6 disciplines. So I filmed some videos and thought I'd see what happens. I put them on YouTube and no one watched them! That didn't stop me though, if I can see the potential in something I go all in and don't stop, which is an attitude I developed through martial arts. So I started filming more videos, and once again no one watched them. I did this for a year or two. Then people started watching them and I started getting some positive comments. I also got some shitty comments, but I kept going anyway!

I then set up the Mittmaster website to advertise and sell the videos and it's taken off! I'm getting people from China, Australia, USA, and all over the world buying and enjoying my videos! This is the great thing about the internet; it allows you to sell to a global market. If I teach a class, I only reach small numbers locally. Online I can teach to the world and only need a few hundred people to like what I'm doing and I can make a living. Unfortunately I can't retire to my yacht yet but it's definitely working! So my next step is to help teach other instructors how to create information products and market them, as martial artists are pretty clueless with this.

What are the plans for the future then in terms of Mittmaster, the business seminars and your own academy?

With Mittmaster I want to build until it becomes known as the best pad training system out there. I then want to teach other instructors how to teach it and spread it further. With my academy, I just want to maintain as I'm happy with where we are with it. On the business side I want to help martial artists. I think there are many good ones out there but they're not reaching people because they don't understand modern marketing. Most martial artists are still martial arts. So I started filming more videos, and once again no one watched them. I did this for a year or two. Then people started watching them and I started getting some positive comments. I also got some shitty comments, but I kept going anyway!

I then set up the Mittmaster website to advertise and sell the videos and it's taken off! I'm getting people from China, Australia, USA, and all over the world buying and enjoying my videos! This is the great thing about the internet; it allows you to sell to a global market. If I teach a class, I only reach small numbers locally. Online I can teach to the world and only need a few hundred people to like what I'm doing and I can make a living. Unfortunately I can't retire to my yacht yet but it's definitely working! So my next step is to help teach other instructors how to create information products and market them, as martial artists are pretty clueless with this.

What are the plans for the future then in terms of Mittmaster, the business seminars and your own academy?

With Mittmaster I want to build until it becomes known as the best pad training system out there. I then want to teach other instructors how to teach it and spread it further. With my academy, I just want to maintain as I'm happy with where we are with it. On the business side I want to help martial artists. I think there are many good ones out there but they're not reaching people because they don't understand modern marketing. Most martial artists are still operating as they did 20 years ago, distributing flyers and wondering why their classes are dead, bemoaning Facebook, the internet and all technology.

If I could help some martial artists free themselves from having to teach classes all the time that would be great. I'm 40 now but don't want to be teaching kids classes when I'm 60, I want to focus on my passion and have a passive sources of income that work while I'm not at the gym. This is a safer way of securing your income rather than just having one source of income (teaching classes). If you're an employee and get laid off it's like 'oh shit', you don't want to be in that position. Same if you're running a class and they close the sports centre you use. That's brown trouser time!

MARTIAL MASTERS Vol 1

It's like going into a fight with just a right cross and hoping it will get you through. You can't be reliant on one source of income, it's risky. If I could help martial artists understand that and leverage their talents so they have multiple sources of income, they'll be safer and I'll be happier!

What has martial arts done for you personally then?

Ah man, it's done everything for me! First of all I've got a really cool job! Other people work in an office and hate it, and I can't imagine spending my life doing something I hate. It's your life, and it can go quick. Why are you spending 8 hours a day doing something you can't stand? WTF that's about? Then you spend the weekend drinking so you can forget about your crap job! Why would you do that to yourself?!

Martial arts have allowed me to do what I want. My mum has always encouraged me to do what I want so when I was 18 and jobless, she would pay for my training while I stayed at home and practised. My mum said "if it's what you want to do, keep doing it." Unfortunately lots of people don't have parents that are that supportive and are more like "get out of the house and get a job, ya layabout!" If my mum had been like that I wouldn't be where I am now. So, thanks Mum.

Martial arts have allowed me to live how I want. I've never had any other job other than martial arts instructor and that's amazing. It's all I've wanted to do and still all I want to do. All I like doing is training and teaching martial arts whether that's classes, business or philosophy. I'm all about sharing my passion, ever since I was a kid. It's all I wanted to do. I didn't want to be a pilot, or join the army, I just wanted to be a martial arts instructor and now I get to do that, and teach others how to! It's great to see kids come up, learn, improve and then open their own clubs.

Martial arts have made me happy throughout my life. My whole approach to life is to only do things that make me happy! I don't want to deal with arseholes at work that hate their job and want to drag you down; I just can't do "normal" jobs! Some people offer excuses, 'well I need the money', or 'I'll stick with it for a while' but hate every minute of it for decades! WHY?! What a terrible thing to do to yourself. Find a way to explore and develop your passion FFS. Life is too damn short to waste your talents doing something you hate.

I only ever followed my bliss and did what I loved and so far it's gone well! I feel very lucky that I had my mum who supported my training and had so many great instructors (Anton St James, Bob Breen, Erik Paulson, and Phil Norman) who believed in me and showed me my potential. And of course there is my awesome business/ training partner James who has been riding along beside me for decades. In the end it's a team effort.

Remember you are the average of the five people you spend the most time with and I'm blessed as I've had so many cool people around me. I'm very thankful for the life that martial arts have allowed me to live! It's been wonderful!

Matthew Chapman

www.mittmaster.com

Andy Norman – Defence Lab

Tony Pillage – Pressure Points

Andy Norman

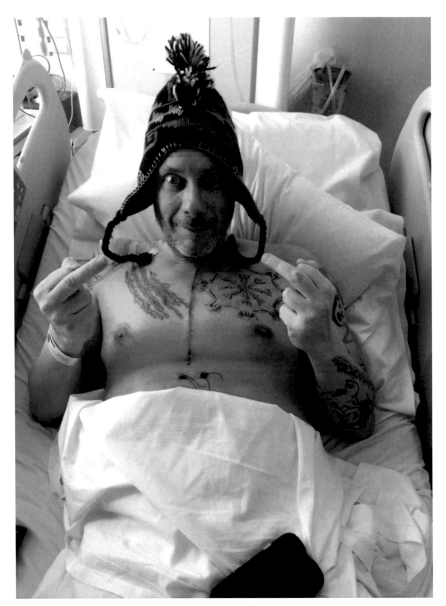

Tony Pillage – just after surgery

Bob Breen with Dan Inosanto

Bob Breen – 4D Combat

Carl Cooper

Dean Williams

Matt Chapman

Dean Williams

Eddie Quinn – The Approach

Eddie Quinn

Matt Chapman

Mick Tully

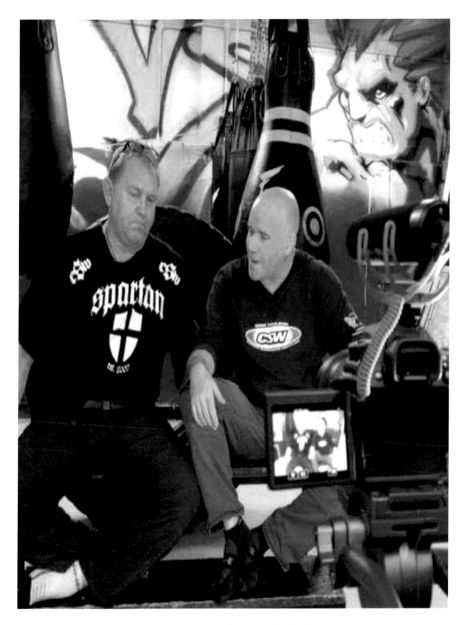

Eric Paulson with Mick Tully

Dan Inosanto with Phil Norman

Phil Norman – Ghost Master

Russell Jarmesty

Russell Jarmesty

Scott Caldwell

Scott Caldwell

Simon Oliver

Simon Oliver

Stewart McGill

Tony Bailey

137

Stewart McGill

Tony Bailey

Zara Phythian – shoot to kill

Zara Phythian – means business

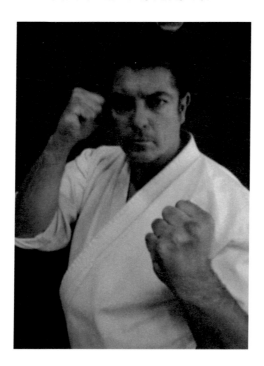

Simon Oliver
Karate

Simon Oliver is a legend in the Karate world with a wealth of experience and knowledge behind making the traditional arts effective for the street. Having trained with some of the best and travelled to Japan on a number of occasions, he's a fantastic and interesting guy to speak to on all things martial arts!

Can you remember when you started martial arts and why?

I started martial arts in 1966 as a little boy under my father's direction as both my father and grandfather were involved with Judo and Ju-Jutsu. My early days were thinking that throwing people around and stuff was fun and play, it's what everybody did.

I got into trouble at school a few times, choking out a few colleagues. It was towards the end of the 60s my father took me to see a martial arts demonstration and that was the first time that I saw karate. It was a group of senior Japanese instructors over from Japan at a place called Alexandra Palace. I saw the demonstration and knew that was what I wanted to do. In those days, there was nobody anywhere that would teach children at all and in fact the national governing body at that time required you to be at least 16 years of age and you had to have references and all sorts, it was quite tough to get in.

I started getting private lessons from a student of Tatsuo Suzuki Sensei. This student of his was a friend of my father's from doing Judo and I was having those private lessons for about 3 years before Suzuki Sensei found out and I was then asked to go and demonstrate my abilities to him down in London. He wouldn't let me train in the normal classes but agreed that Pete Bell who I had been having the privates from could carry on teaching me. I didn't actually get into a formal class until the early 70's and we moved house where I was then taught by a guy called Alan Rushby. Alan was one of the first Shukokai instructors based up in Doncaster and the power this little short stocky guy could produce was incredible. God could this guy could move but he looked like a Mexican Bandit. Due to my father's job we moved again and I ended up back more North near Liverpool where I had lived originally. That's where I first met Terry O'Neill Sensei and to say I was in awe of him, I think I was more terrified. This guy just amazed me and I started training with him. What I didn't realise was that I'd stumbled on one of the most open martial arts instructors around at that time and I was exposed to many different arts through Terry.

I was involved at that time in the Shotokan camp, competing and enjoying training, but there was also something in the back of my mind questioning as I had started working nightclub doors. I started to realise that it wasn't really designed for what I wanted to do and there were gaps. Terry's way of teaching was very pragmatic and sensible however and he was a real character. He was the only guy who I had seen tell people what he was going to hit them with out on the street, then actually manage to hit them with it. I'm still in total admiration. The man is nearly 70 and still standing on nightclub doors in Liverpool, following 2 hip replacements and a knee replacement. He'll always be my Sensei as he instilled in me this openness to look at any martial art and look for the similarities and connecting points, the areas of overlap that allowed a common ground to work on.

This gave me the ability to go and train with anybody and gain information from anybody. So when I ended up in Japan for the first time, I trained at the JKA, enjoyed it, but realised that it was a place they were breeding athletes. The direction in the 70s and 80s was obvious with one element of karate being very sport driven, but the other element was sort of disappearing.

When I asked senior instructors about this style of training they described it as Koryu or old style and I was lucky enough to be put in touch with 2 instructors who taught the old style. One called Shinkin Gima and another Sensei called Yasuhiro Konishi and to say they revolutionised my ideas about martial arts was to put it mildly. I concentrated on training with Konishi Sensei who was an amazing individual. He started as a Kendo instructor and Ju-Jutsu practitioner. Then went to Karate under Funakoshi then moved to the often maligned Choki Motobu. And Motobu was the real fighter and it was obvious Konishi blended those experiences together to come up with his own system called Shindo-Jinen-Ryu which is very much a jutsu system; it's not designed for sport really. Its instruction is fundamentally for self-defence which I use in the most loose term. I found it was a system for self-development. He amazed me because he first saw Westerners arrive, looked at them and then enrolled in the local boxing academy to learn how they move and learn to fight them. He then became one of the top boxing coaches in Japan and trained some of the top fighters.

I came back from Japan after that first visit and didn't really realise who I'd been training with. I got stuck into training with a lot of the Shotokan boys but was starting to deviate way off the standard syllabus due to the things I'd been shown about application and how to apply the concept of Bunkai Oyo Henka, my training was becoming more related to developing individuals rather than a group class environment. I think if the MMA thing had arrived earlier for me I would have just gone straight into that.

I ended up sort of trying to evolve what I had been taught by Konishi and his senior student Yamazaki Sensei but stayed within the group I was involved with for many years. It wasn't until the late 90s that I really decided to make the permanent switch and started teaching from the direction I'd been given on the several trips to Japan which was a lot more practically orientated. I found myself aligning with people who had got to the cross training principle from various different routes and suddenly felt more at home with that ideology.

I wear a Gi still as it's psychologically good for me and I'd never move from the Japan Karate-do Ryobukai as it gives me the spectrum of training that I want to work with and the self-expression that I want. We're all martial artists and we're therefore being creative in a martial sense. If we're not, we die and if it doesn't move and change with the environment it dies too.

I always remember something that Steve Morris said many years ago where he said there are many people putting on the tiger's skin, but not actually becoming the tigers themselves but not realising how close they are. What he was saying is that just by changing some of your training principles you become a lot more effective instead of just looking good. That was never an issue to me, I never looked nice doing karate anyway, and I'd been on the front end and had got plenty of experience on what really works. What I wanted to do was make my training relate to what I needed and that changes as you get older.

When I was in my 20s I was probably less civilised in some respects, and I was dealing in a different environment. By the time I was in my late 40s my training was more related to where I was in my life and my health. Certainly now I'm in my late 50s, I'm still teaching different people of different age groups to be confident in their ability. I want them to stand up and be counted by themselves. I want them to work within society. If it's just about punching and kicking, it's going to be a very negative experience at the end, the punching and kicking also has to make us better people at the end of it. Better physical specimens and better emotional specimens. We all have our ups and downs in life and I think that's my direction today.

What was it about Karate that instantly drew you?

I'd never seen people moving so dynamically when it came to striking and kicking. It was the dynamics of it that interested me more than anything else. Of course, coming from a grappling background I was used to how people moved when you grabbed them and how to throw and pin people, what I'd never seen was that sort of striking. It didn't have to have been karate, if I'd seen Thai Boxing at that time maybe it would have had the same influence, it was just at the time Karate was being promoted heavily. Even with the big Kung Fu boom in the 1970s, the Japanese martial arts benefitted more and had the biggest group and established structures in place. It seemed a natural progression to move into Karate for me as I wanted that ability to kick and punch people like that. Now as I look back I've seen the footage from that demo and now realise from the knowledge I have now that it was acting, a demo, but still inspiring enough to grab me enough at that age.

From day one it was always self-defence orientated for me. I wasn't a great specimen physically as a little kid and didn't start growing until later in my teens. I come from a diverse ethnic background which meant I was ideal bully material and so both my father and grandfather were keen I could look after myself.

I remember reading an article not so long ago by Lyoto Machida's father saying that after his first fight in the cage his father said that you now know how it feels to be truly alone. I had a great childhood, I was bullied which was predictable as I had a bit of a mouth on me but from day one in the martial arts training it was about self-defence. The Ju-Jutsu was taught as self-defence, it wasn't taught as a psychological benefitting exercise, it was taught as a self defence system.

Did that teaching translate well into your experiences of real life self-defence?

As I got older, it became very natural to me and I realised I had a skill set that was very easy to use, not just for self-defence but also for protecting other people. Some people develop skill sets earlier on which enable them to do all sorts of things and I'm a bit of a freak as I had that early martial arts training it had become the norm to react. I didn't realise it but that concept of Shu-Ha-Ri. I'd actually got through the first stage and was in the second stage of actually making it work for me. People may not ride a bike for a while, but once you've learnt, you've learnt and it doesn't take you long to get back into the idea of it. Martial arts became a natural way of expressing myself and so then when I began to compete many years later it was a natural way for me to express myself and it felt right. Teaching is the same for me and I think a lot of people teach because they're forced into it. I actually enjoy it and like seeing people improve both physically and mentally and to actually see a change in them as human beings I find rewarding and a big achievement. I think as a martial artist that's what martial arts has given me, that ability to appeal to a certain group, but also the confidence to communicate to others who have nothing to do with martial arts. If a martial artist can walk in the room and talk and communicate with people without intimidating them, that's important.

How were your competition days?

I think I competed during the golden age of competition. It was the decline of my senior's careers in the early 80s, but the emerging of a new scene. The actual open championships where you'd see many different martial arts groups ready to compete became the vogue of the early 80s and I have to admit I enjoyed competition. I won both kata and kumite competitions and I think my greatest win was an open over in Holland. It was more fun to me; it was a day off because I was involved in the security business for a long time so it was just a day off. I didn't take it too seriously though which was probably my downfall as I didn't maintain a lot of consistency, it didn't matter to me if I won or lost, it mattered if I enjoyed it. I sometimes think I should have taken it more seriously, but it was never going to be my bag, but it did give me a whole array of friends all over the world and people who I still talk to on a regular basis 40 years later. Time has gone so quickly and the great thing is seeing them still around and not just training but giving something back to the martial arts as well.

Tell us about some of your experiences on the doors

I started working on the doors quite young. I'd just turned 18 and it was out of necessity rather than desire and I have to admit it was a rude awakening. I remember standing on the first door in Nottingham during the Miner's Strikes and during that time it wasn't particular miners you were fighting it was more different police officers from different constabularies. It was a rough and tumble kind of time. Dealing with someone compromised by alcohol or drugs, you soon realise you have to be able to break structure and you have to do it quick. You have to be decisive and take control or it will escalate and other people are likely to get injured.

I can remember one distinct instance of a club in Nottingham where I was working with another Karate guy who was obviously very talented. We got locked outside of the nightclub having expelled 4 individuals who had then regrouped with 8 others and come back. We then had to fight our way out of the situation and it became a lesson in how to use the environment such as dustbin lids. New dustbin lids are not designed for good self-defence but the old ones were!

I quickly realised that some of the skill sets that I had gained from the martial arts were great in certain environments, but would be a great hindrance in others. One of the biggest lessons I learnt was how to use my mouth to diffuse situations. Getting into a fight is the last thing you want when there's more than one individual. Size helps, but skill set will save your life most definitely. Being direct, decisive and being first is really important and I learnt that lesson very hard. I tried to talk somebody down once, and this person wasn't having it and before I realised it they were on me and what they wanted to do was fight. Under pressure, you resort to what you know well and I realised that it wasn't the Karate that saved me; it was the Ju-Jutsu. I'd spun this guy and choked him out before I had a chance to strike him so I realised some of the stuff I learned very early on was of great value. 6 months later I got into another altercation and I remember kicking someone with a front kick from close up and that worked for me.

I realised quickly that certain things wouldn't work for me. I've seen stuff pulled off from certain individuals that I'd never try, just because I didn't have the confidence in the technique but they did and could pull it off. I tended to be very short, sharp and direct and line people up from an angle to avoid their second assault. 9 out of 10 times when people attack, they attack with everything they have. Violence is violence no matter what you say sometimes the only response is violence back, it's the only way a situation can be stopped. You need to know when to do that and the greatest experience I think I got from those days was having that skill set of realising when it's time to go and not hold back or you're going to hospital.

There are some tremendously skilled people out there teaching lots of stuff, but for those in the know they look at them and go, I don't think you've ever had a fight. Would you go to a driving instructor who has never driven a car on the road? You wouldn't even get in the car with them? I think everyone should have some experience. If you look back as far as warriors being taught by warriors, if you're going to teach people how to look after themselves you need some experience. You wouldn't put a soldier into the battlefield unless they've been trained by someone who has had that experience and knows the mental aspect too. I've been to some seminars and you can tell the people who have real experience as they're honest and talk about the fear. I also see others being honest and saying I've never had a fight or worked on a door, I suppose you have the choice. Stay away from people who bastardize the art just solely for money though, that has always been a guideline. If you're going to teach people how to look after themselves you need some real world experience.

What do you think about the current state of martial arts in the UK and abroad?

I like what I see on the whole. There is more choice and I like that there are people out there not getting hung up on names, titles, grades, they're just training. To a certain extent that's a blast in to the past as in the early days that's what people did. I think that's a good thing, but I do see a huge division happening and to a certain extent I'm not against it. I see some moving heavily to sport martial arts; I see it happening with karate like it did with taekwondo. I think there's space there for it and if people want to do it let them do it.

What I get concerned about is when people then try and sell that as self-defence. I'm a great admirer of athletes, however, and that's what these guys are. I think there's a happy middle ground. For me as I get older, I can't do either end any more. I'm too old for the sporting end and I'm too old to get in the cage. I'm carrying way too many injuries but I admire the guys that do it. I have a number of students of mine who have got into it and I'll always support and go and watch them. I found a middle ground which works for me. It allows me to train and be reality based, that connection to the reality based groups in Japan that were pre-war is my influence, that works for me! For world martial arts, these divisions are not going to go away and I can see that there is probably going to be this big divide between the sports martial arts against the reality based martial arts and then there's going to be a grey area in the middle. What does scare me, I'm not against anybody earning a living, but the get rich quick schemes which are business models. That's a process of self-delusion that is going on and that scares me. That's the one thing I'm really uncomfortable about.

I like the two extreme ends and I like the people who are in the middle area finding the ability to manage both worlds. I'm really against someone giving a relative novice a black belt with a white stripe and saying you're now an apprentice instructor, it's risky for the individual getting the belt and also for the students that follow that regime. I'd like the extreme ends to get their marketing as good as some of these guys as some of them are really struggling for income, but they have great messages.

Some of these business models are doing very well, but they're business models and sometimes it's hard to tell that to the general public. You'd think after all the years martial arts have been around and how much they are bombarded to us in the media, people would get the idea and be able to spot the fakes but it hasn't happened yet. We're seeing that we still need to educate people. But as a whole I think this is a magic time, as people have choices, great choices and there are some great people out there teaching.

I'm a martial art nerd, I love them all. If I see someone training I'll go and speak to them, ask what they're doing and how it works. I don't care where they came from or what it is, it doesn't matter to me. I have always been wary of the instructor that demands complete loyalty and retards his student's evolution. So today, to a certain extent I'm happier than I probably was in the 70s and the fact is people have more choices now and fewer restrictions.

Martial arts and business can go hand in hand but it's down to the individual. They can work out and as I said there are certain business models that worry me as they're not honest. I think first of all as a martial artist you have to be honest, to yourself and to your students. I think there are business models that do work. We've gone past the days where someone can come and see you for some training in exchange for 3 chickens; society doesn't work that way anymore, at the moment the world runs on currencies. Therefore, people have bills to pay and if you are offering integrity and honesty then I think martial arts and business can go hand in hand. There are some great people out there running good gyms and offering quality, they're being honest. I listen to the messages they put out and they're honest and I think that's the important thing.

What do you think it takes to be a good instructor?

As I've got older I think you change. I think these days the most important thing is a good set of ears for an instructor. Too many instructors tell people stuff instead of listening. Everybody who walks in your dojo has a story and a need. Some people you can't help and if you don't listen to them you won't know. Others you can help but you'll only know that if you listen and watch. Actions speak louder than words but you do have to listen to people and watch how they move and interact. That will give a clue about the quality of the individuals around you. There are many times that I've changed teaching strategies around a group of individuals or an individual. I've moved away from the concept of thinking you can teach a class of people. Even in a class you still need to spend time with individuals. I don't like big classes and see courses with 400 people on and it would scare me to death. I couldn't teach a class like that and don't think I'd be giving quality as I'd be wearing an ear piece and addressing hundreds of people. When I go to seminars, if I got one thing from attending it was worth the money, if I got two, it was worth being there, if I got three, then that's someone I want to train with more often, that's what I always thought when training so I try and think like that when teaching now. I always get people to critique my seminars and tell me things they like and what they didn't like, so I can improve.

Teaching is a two way thing. When I was training in Japan, at the beginning of the class we bow to each other and say `onegaishimasu` which means please teach me. We say it to each other. The teacher to the student, the student back to the teacher. That's why I still partner up with people even with my injuries! I need to remember I'm in my late 50s now and not a young boy and I therefore progress by that interaction. I have to tone it down a little bit due to the injuries, but you still need to interact with people on a contact basis or you won't progress. You'll still progress as you get older, you never stop learning.

At least twice a week I'll get in there and physically do stuff, and I'll do more if I can, otherwise you stagnate. When I have other instructors come and teach, I don't sit there just collecting the fees, I get my Gi on and train. It's respectful and it's good for me. It's to learn to respect other people and other's ideas. You may not always agree, but if you don't respect you're limiting yourself. There are a lot of blinkered people in the martial arts and I hate saying this but some of them are from the very orthodox backgrounds and I think if you just lifted the blinkers for half an hour, you'd really get the sunlight coming in.

What about the future then?

I hope I'm still around in 10 years and still doing stuff. For me, the greatest thing is seeing my own students move on and do things for themselves and create their own identities for themselves in whatever walk of life they decide to go down. As long as it's positive and beneficial to them and the rest of society it's good with me.

For me as a martial artist I'm just going to keep on doing what I'm doing, the minute I stop enjoying it is the minute I stop. I've had my ups and downs, real low times, but the only thing that's kept me going is the fact that I can get in the dojo and punch, kick and spar with somebody, then all of a sudden the world isn't such a bad place and it's a kind of positive therapy. It's always been through my whole life, the balance, the place of the way, by that, it's the place for me that was consistent. If I got too big for my boots, it was a place to put me down. If I was going through crap it was a place I could go to escape then in the morning, get up and deal with it. As long as I can keep doing that then I can keep putting stuff back into the martial arts and back into the students so the future is looking good.

There are plenty of people I want to train with so I'm hoping the body will last! There are lots of people I've met over the past couple of years, thanks to social media, that fascinate me and I want to train and experience that training with them. It all just interests me! I experienced the Gracie's a few years ago, long before they were starting to hit the big time and that's an experience I'd like to do again, they had bugger all when I first trained with them, except a lot of talent, determination, a way of training and philosophy that was enjoyable. There are a lot of people out there that I admire and I want to train with and for as long as I can!

Zara Phythian
PBA Academy

Zara is a leading film actress and instructor at the Personal Best Academy (PBA). She has most recently starred in *Dr Strange* alongside Benedict Cumberbatch and is a 13 times multi style sports martial arts champion.

A talented martial artist, actress, performer and business woman it was a pleasure to interview her as a rising star in the martial arts world.

Let's start at the beginning on when you began martial arts.

I started just as I turned 7 years old. My father took me to a local martial arts class that was running in the area. My family (I have 3 sisters) have always had sport in their blood since their early years, mainly swimming but my sister Zoe was already taking classes at the place so I was bought along. I wasn't very sporty at the time so I don't think anyone thought I would take the classes seriously. The class was Shotokan Karate which I studied up to 2nd Degree black belt in at the age of 14.

Can you remember how you felt walking in to your first class?

It was so long ago I don't really recall too many memories of those early introductions to martial arts. One think I do know was that I was quite a reserved child, not very outgoing, I would say lacking in confidence. I was quiet but just did my thing, it was quite hardcore traditional looking back on it and sometimes I was the only young girl training among not only boys but grown men. I took it quite seriously looking back, and was quite aggressive! Whether that was me trying to fit in among the rest of the class I don't know, but I remember early Shotokan tournaments where I was disqualified for too much contact – my Dad was really quite proud of that!!

Even at that time, I was established in my school but I really didn't know much about martial arts, just the association and club I guess. As I got older and spread out it actually struck me that after 7 years of training with a particular association, I never even realised that Sensei Asano and people like the amazing Adrian Trimble were actually based less than half a mile around the corner! That said, it was a good school and based a solid foundation for me for my years that followed in martial arts. The school was run by the

Tucker brothers, a good start to Karate I feel and I do believe the school still runs under the name of `Wandering Dragon`.

When did you know that martial arts were going to be something you would do for the rest of your life?

Good question! I would say in my teens, just about when I was ready to leave school and head for college. As I said, I had been introduced to the world of martial arts. I had a friend who had just come back from a Kickboxing tournament which he had won, he mentioned to my dad about a school that sounded incredible to us, so we went along for a trial session and that was the start of a life changing experience although we didn't know it at the time.

The school was called the Nottingham School of Champions and was a full time academy with mats, bags – all the gear! I remember being in awe of the place and the instructors and students (100s of them) when I first started there. I was totally hooked and that's when I realised I actually liked martial arts rather than just being good at it. The place had a strong traditional foundation to it, something I was comfortable with, but also had this incredible modern approach and diversity that I had not experienced. Something a teenage girl could easily fit in to without losing the integrity of what we are there for.

I began to study Tae Kwon Do both sport and traditional, as well as Kickboxing and Combative Reality combat methods. From training twice a week in a local school hall drilling kata, I was unleashed to training up to 5 times a week cross training. I learnt so much in such a short time. I thought I could kick, and then found out how to kick effectively. I thought I could hit, and then got hit and realised I better step my game up! After a couple of initial years there I realised, 'yes this is my life, my way, I couldn't imagine doing anything else.' Be it tournaments, testing for new black belts or just being on an open mat training, this was my way, this is what I do.

You're a Multisport Martial Arts World Champion; talk a little to us about your days competing and how you felt walking into your first competition.

Competition days really started for me when I had established myself at the School of Champions. The first couple of years focused on fighting only and I loved to fight. Again, a big eye opener for me with the vast amount of open tournaments and different styles present! Remember I was used to the closed traditional practice so all the atmosphere of open tournaments was a real buzz to me.

Within my first year of competing, I went to my first international open and really didn't know what to expect! My dad went with me too and I was so nervous as with us were experienced team mates such as Owen King and Clifton Findley. I can remember one fight where I was beating a local German fighter. I was my usual aggressive (not undisciplined) self, I can't even recall to this day what kicked off but I seemed to have enraged the coach/parent of the other fighter. Next thing I knew I had a bottle thrown at me! It got a little heated out there and I think the promoters of the event kicked them out of the building but I was so focused on the fight it all went a little over my head. I wasn't and still am not sure what I actually did to upset them, but I was hooked from the banter you get from team mates of such high calibre.

I really liked the international circuit experience and the rest was history really. Through different associations, but always representing the School of Champions, I continued to compete at

Worlds and Internationals and was fortunate to do this successfully in places like USA, Jamaica, Mexico and all around Europe. I also returned back to kata and forms, as well as always fighting. In this country, that gave me the edge with regards to making a name for myself because here you either did kata or you were a point fighter. In the USA this is normal, so both myself and fellow team mate, Kayley Marke, were well equipped for tournaments in the States as we did and were successful in various disciplines such as traditional kata, Tae Kwon Do patterns, point fighting, Kickboxing continuous, weapons and extreme musical forms. It made us different and we always had a bunch more trophies to take home, along with different experiences we could get from just the one discipline.

I would also say that it made us appreciative of the diversity of martial arts more, furthered our understanding and so multi-discipline competition was a good thing for me. Some of the best experiences in martial arts for me have come from my time in International competitions.

How do you relate martial arts and self defence? Do they differ for you?

I guess everyone has a different opinion on this one. For me, martial arts are simply that, the martial arts. There is something for everyone, not just those who want to get fit, those who want to compete, those who want self defence or those who feel captured by the essence and culture of martial arts.

I've been so fortunate to have had the opportunity to train in sports, traditional and reality – I love it all and it all has its purpose. I must say thought that I don't like comparisons, I think it's pointless, there is so much lack of martial arts respect around these days in my opinion for each other's practice of what they do and this to me is really sad. Martial arts are awesome, diverse and ever evolving. There is a lot more out there for people to choose from if they want to benefit from training and that's what's important to me – the benefits rather than who's better, what's better etc. What I would say though is the term `self defence` needs to be used these days with more thought. I'm not saying let's say if you start a traditional style like Shotokan Karate that you shouldn't advertise it as self defence to people, but because a lot of modern schools have watered down what they used to teach and the reason for teaching it.

Today's society is increasingly growing with violence so we should all look at what we say and promote as self defence. The same goes for reality based styles or systems. Too many times I hear a reality instructor or student saying a sports martial artist can't fight on the street. What a load of rubbish! How do they know?! Have they seen them fight on the street? No. I've seen guys come to a class who are pretty tasty in a stereotypical way when it comes to being street savvy, yet can't last 20 seconds with a Kickboxer. So what if that guy ends up 20 seconds in a street fight with a Kickboxer, maybe he doesn't win now?

There is a massive difference between reality and matted I do understand that, but there are also ways to complement both in one's training. I'll probably get hate messages for this next bit too. I'm known to not be too keen on women only self defence and a lot of people raise their eyebrows at this so I want to take this opportunity to say what I mean. I agree when people say a lot of women aren't confident enough to go to a mixed class. Street defence is scary, really scary and doing mixed classes with sweaty men can put a lot of ladies off. That said, a male or female attacker doesn't care, has no boundaries, and let's face it a woman's most feared attacker is a man. So I don't tend to follow the women only self defence thing that much, but along with that I also think we need more female reality type instructors out there. Male instructors also need to understand and feel the fears that a woman has in attack. Like I said, self defence for me is a word that needs thought sometimes but I do feel it falls under the martial arts banner. Just my opinion folks!

What do you think to the current state of martial arts in the UK and abroad?

It's terrible, everyone is rubbish, and I'm the best thing ever! OK, just joking!

I guess this is the `McDojo` question? For me I look at how martial arts have grown around the world and in the media. How the sports side is becoming more mainstream, especially MMA/UFC, the rapid growth of reality systems and participants. The traditional schools are on the up too. Karate goes into the Olympics; it's all growth because more and more are participating in some form of martial arts. I don't see that as a bad thing because I love martial arts and want everyone else to love it too. All that said, yes there are a lot more poorer standards being seen these days and in many opinions, far too much emphasis on giving our black belts for far less skill level or effort than before because of the business side. But I don't really go for the McDojo slating argument. Are we just seeing more of what some people see as poor standards due to 1) Social media 2) More schools? Did we have poor standard schools back when I was a kid, sure we did, just because it was the matter of someone's opinion of what should be and shouldn't be, doesn't make them right. Just an opinion!

I believe in the martial arts business aspects. The marketing, the retention skills, the full time school. I do believe people can run very successful martial arts school financially and remain true to the standard that they set for their students. It's down to what they set, not someone else's opinion however because if that's so then I'm a McDojo and so are many friends and legends in the arts because someone always thinks they are better than you or their school is. I'm not one for having a go at the McDojo's because quite simply I don't know what one is. I'm not going to lie, there is a lot of weird rubbish going on, and you see it nearly every week on Facebook! There are some cults like things going on as well in martial arts, but it's like everything, as soon as the industry grows branches off it, out come all sorts of things! I think the current state of martial arts as a whole is brilliant, but we seem to only want to talk about the McDojo elements and opinions, we don't show enough of what matters which is the martial arts and the good stuff. Take this book, we are all different. I'm sure when I read it there will be lots of different opinions. Some I will share, some I won't, but it's a positive take on martial arts I hope, showing the diversity, all the different knowledge and experience. Is everyone in this book everyone's cup of tea? I doubt it but it doesn't matter, because we are someone's cup of tea, someone's high standard and someone's inspiration. Martial arts are growing every year and we are all part of it. Yes the standard is good in my opinion, but I focus on what I think is good, not on what I think is poor!

What do you think to the current level of female martial artists?

I think its top class! I really mean that, so inspiring. When I was coming through in the early days of training, I really didn't know of many household type female names. Now there's loads and it's growing, just look at the likes of Rhonda Rousey and all she has done for female MMA. Women are involved in all the martial arts these days and being just as successful as men and in many cases (but not enough yet) as respected as men are. These days you even see more women school owners all around the country, that's got to tell you about the growth of female martial arts. In sports martial arts, women are as dominant as men now in the tournament scene. Just going back to my thoughts on self defence, in particular women's self defence. If you look at all the top sports, reality and traditional female martial artists, how many of them trained in a `women only` format? It really is great to see more and more women in martial arts and the standard is great too, but then again why wouldn't it be?

Tell us about how you first decided to open your own school PBA and how your programme was received.

I opened the first PBA Academy 9 ½ years ago. A friend couldn't run his gym anymore and we decided that after my years of experience running one of the full time branches of the School of Champions that I could possibly go and start a new business at his gym and open an academy. It was always going to be a challenge. It was in the town of Mansfield, there was a strong number of martial arts classes there historically but no full time schools, so when I went to open the school I got a lot of feedback from other schools, mainly that it wouldn't work in Mansfield. Plus there were no female instructors so how could one come and open a full time school – they were pretty set in their ways. But I had the experience of Vic and the School of Champions with me. I had no capital, no loans, just a high rent, bits of equipment that already came with the gym some sponsor help from Quality Martial Arts and more importantly NO students from day one. If anyone ever asked me advice about opening a full time school and they were in my situation I would probably advise against it, after all the previous gym hadn't worked out either.

I know instructors are proud of their schools and I'm no different but I love the PBA and what we have achieved over the years within the Mansfield community so much, I'm so proud. Fast forward 9 years and where are we at? Well there are now 6 other full time martial arts schools in Mansfield, some I'm sure were ones that said not here, that won't happen! I now have 2 full time schools in the town, including what I believe is still Britain's first and only children only full time academy open only to 4-12 year olds, home to nearly 200 of that age! We are also headquarters for Team England (WMKF)

I don't compete with other schools locally, in fact the more that open the better, our industry is growing. I'm really fortunate to have a great team of instructors here who promote our ethos. Yes we are modern, some would say McDojo, but we keep our traditional values, we are very strong on discipline and respect the old way and combine it with a modern approach. We have a lifestyle here that we are proud of.

How did you first get introduced into the acting world?

It was completely by chance. I was in Cleveland competing for the USA National Title Belt Open and winning I might add 4 title belts! Anyway, over there they had this talent competition running on the mats at the same time I was competing on the forms areas next to it. It was all a bit weird to us British competitors because we didn't have that type of division in Europe. I wasn't really paying too much attention to it, basically it's like a forms and self defence competition but with the judges actually being filmmakers and producers. I was performing 9 section whip chain in the weapons division which was always a crowd stopper over there (not often you see whip chain performed by a non-oriental female). Apparently whilst performing they stopped the other area because the judges/producers were fixed on what I was doing, then after receiving first place I was approached by some local filmmakers. One in particular, George Butriti, a Cleveland based filmmaker gave me his card and wondered if I would be interested in his film he was making. It was seen as a joke at the time, because anyone that knew me knew you couldn't even get me for pictures let alone video at competitions. I hated cameras plus had no experience or desire to be in stunts let alone acting. Anyway, after returning back to England, he got in contact a few times, pitching the script and the plan. It was then that I realised he had written a character role in there for me called `Snipe` a kick ass take no prisoners female soldier that was part of an elite team. It was a low budget sci-fi, it had US soap actors in it and I wasn't too confident in doing it but we decided what the hell, another chance to go back stateside and kick butt!

So I spent a couple of months living there doing this film. I was hopeless at the start, but the cast were amazing! I began to grow on set, learn on the spot about character development. Of course the action was easy, the acting though, that was hard (and still is)! I travelled to the States twice to complete the film and then for the screening. Although it was low budget it was such a great experience and the friends I made are for life.

I loved the Cleveland filmmaking network over there, met others from other films being made and I was totally hooked! A complete surprise to both myself and my family so when I got back I started to look at getting in to the UK filmmaking circuit. From that I got straight on to the film *Underground* and realised we had our own indie filmmaking industry here. Then came the odd music video casting and more low budget action work.

A lot of the big names on the martial arts tournament circuit I noticed were getting on big films in the stunt area, but they were stunt registered and I took advice from a friend who was doing very well in resisting the stunt register and being seen as an actor. That's what I wanted to do, so I did! I still got to work on stunts and do double work, but not as much. It's a great living though, but I love the new challenge of acting, not because I want to be in front of the camera but because I like the development of character and the different roles. Everyone that knew me back then including myself could have never imagined me not competing on the circuit, but I made the decision once I was hooked that I needed to spend time and focus on acting and the film industry if I wanted to be involved more, and that as they say, is history. I stopped competing in 2006/2007.

When would you say your big break came?

My real break in terms of being seen as an actress rather than martial artist being in films was the horror film from Lions Gate called *The Hike*. Somehow I had landed the female role and I was so determined to do this, even though I know I didn't have enough acting experience. By now I had done a couple of features and mainly music videos and some TV appearance work too, but that was all performance action related, this was about acting, emotional acting too! Once again, I got lucky, the cast were amazing, so talented and didn't hold my lack of experience against me. It was a real team film, it got worldwide DVD release and got me noticed in the horror genre which was nice because it wasn't me kicking and punching and gave me a bit more substance as an actress. Yes, I wanted to act in action films, but wanted to be hired as an actress, not only stunts. The film wasn't the biggest budget, but it got me on the radar. After that I think it was *He Who Dares* where I play a terrorist, then *Transit 17,* back to the action but I'd learned a lot from *The Hike*. I owe the producers and director so much on that movie!

What has it been like working on *Dr Strange* in the recent months?

I'd just got off the back of working on two large budget mainstream films but they were in the stunts department so I understood the big movie mentality and how things worked, but this job was my first actor role on such a movie scale and wow was it an experience! It totally made me realise I made the right decision following this path in my life; I'm actually having the interview for this book out here in Hollywood in sunny LA! I guess by the time this is read, the film will be out but I'm still under contract with Marvel whilst giving you an answer so I'll have to keep it wrapped up a little with no spoilers!

My role meant I'd be working with stunts a lot, as well as production and cast. What an honour it was, seriously, the experience was amazing. The months leading up to the final shooting were old school hard work and the physical conditioning they had us go through was amazing! I was buzzed because it was like I was allowed to train again, learn again so it was all good! Then we got to start working with A-list actors! What an incredible experience, all of them treating you as part of the team, no ego's, pure talent! Laughs, banter, and the seriousness of getting down to business makes this film really something special. All *Dr Strange* has done is make me want to act more and yes, it has all the perks of big budget and as an actress you have to love that!

That's not what inspires you though. It's working with such amazing actors and learning from them, that's what makes you want to do more. I have been so fortunate to get the role I have, I love being part of this project and really can't wait to see the final cut. I've seen snippets, but I haven't seen it all together yet! Would I want to do it again? Of course! But equally it's a tough industry, so I made sure I took all the experience of it while I was on set with amazing actors. All we can hope for is the film to do well and everyone enjoy the on screen experience!

What are your plans for the future then?

I'm hoping to open a new large full time martial art centre which will not only include the programmes we already provide under the PBA Banner, but also a large MMA element and gym. At this time we are in talks so hopefully we move forward on this soon! I'm also looking at licensing the PBA brand nationally to possibly open more schools and develop more businesses for school owners which I hope would begin in 2017.

I'm also currently working on a new film with director James Bushe, a horror comedy called *Cannibals and Carpet Fitters,* a feature version of the award winning short film. Plus I start work shortly on *Knights of the Damned*; once again I get to work with *The Hike* producer and friend Ben L Holmes so can't wait for it, it looks epic! In 2017 my husband Vic makes his feature film producer debut with the film *Lady Dragon* which I'm totally dedicated to. I'm working closely with Sifu Samuel Kwok on the choreography on this with some amazing Wing Chun elements so I can't wait to get started on that either!

Carl Cooper
Toxic Fighting System

Carl has a rich background in martial arts with a speciality in Krav Maga. When he began to notice he was doing more of his own thing, he developed the Toxic Fighting System which has been well received through his DVD set and various seminars across the world. Featured regularly in MAI magazine as well as a number of other publications, Toxic is a great system for personal safety and protection. Here's Carl's story:

It all began on the 7th of April 1969 when I was born to Michael and Carol Cooper in a hospital in London E13.

As I grew up I was never the biggest kid in the class in fact the complete opposite. I was the small scrawny ginger headed kid. The kind who always wore his sleeves down so that people couldn't see how thin his arms were. All I really needed to complete the

ultimate 'Walking punch bag look' was some NHS glass, repaired with a piece of sticking plaster.
As such I was often the 'go to' guy if you needed someone to pick on. Now over time this obviously takes away any self-confidence you may have. And that can be hard to shake off, even in later life.

Initially the bullying began in the latter years of junior school and then continued all throughout secondary school.

Now being that I grew up in the seventies and early eighties there was not too much known about Martial Arts and to my knowledge at that time there were not many Martial Arts clubs around either, although there probably were. It wasn't like nowadays where you can google Martial Arts clubs and pages after pages of Martial Arts clubs appear. So many were found from newspaper adverts, posters or word of mouth.

On the TV I could only ever really remember the TV series *Kung Fu* (I was a little too young to watch that). And then there was *Hong Kong Phooey,* a cartoon series about a mild mannered janitor called Henry. So my knowledge about the Martial Arts around that time was very limited.

But all that changed when I was eleven. I started secondary school and I met someone there who had just found a Karate Club and he asked if I wanted to come along.

Of course I wanted to go. I was 11 and I wanted to wear the white suit and get to Black Belt. I was proud to trot along from home to class wearing my uniform, even if all I had to start with was a white belt. This was a little chance for me to get a bit of escapism, to build up some confidence away from school. But as with many of my friends who ever came along to Martial Arts classes with me he quit after a few months and I carried on going.

I carried on until I got to blue belt. I lost interest by then as it was all katas and no sparring. This was probably because of our age, as the adults were allowed to spar. So after leaving that club I stopped for a couple of years. As I said there weren't many clubs around so you couldn't just go from club to club.

Well things changed in 1985. I started work and I got a renewed interest in Martial Arts. There was a newsagents next to Tonbridge Station that used to sell Martial Arts magazines from America. These had impressive articles and adverts that promised things like "How to develop forearms like a Ninja" and such like. As a 16 year old YTS plumbing apprentice I was impressed. I used to show my boss the magazines and he took up martial arts as well. We would often be seen jumping out on each other and fighting like Kato and Inspector Clouseau from the *Pink Panther* films. Due to Health and Safety on building sites you couldn't do that these days.

Also around this time another friend of mine had a cousin who went to Aikido. It was about 10 miles each way from where I lived. But it was OK because his cousin had a car and he would drive us to and from lessons. This worked out really well until he moved away to Hastings.

My friend decided he would give up at the same time but I wanted to keep going. Now my Dad had friends at work who lived in the village where the classes were held and so I used to have walk to my Dad's workplace to meet his friends and they would drive me to class. Then later that evening my Dad would drive out to collect me.

This was the only time my parents ever showed any interest in my Martial Arts training.
I carried on the training in Aikido and because I used to arrive so early for class my instructor used to get me to help out with the children's classes.

Then a big turning point happened for me when I turned 18 I met John Carrigan. Now this man changed the way I viewed Martial Arts. He was a JKD instructor and this was the nearest thing I had seen to what I used to read in the American magazines. No disrespect to the Martial Arts I had learnt before but they hadn't really given me back much of the confidence I had lost through bullying. It may just have been an age thing, as I was still only around 18 years old. But I could see something completely different here, something I really wanted to learn. Something that I thought would be useful to me.

Around the same time aged 18 or 19 I used to play 5-a-side football. I was the eldest in the team as it was mostly made up of my brother's friends who were two years younger than me. We played in an adult football league and as such we could be 'bullied' a bit. I used to play in goal and as such I was only allowed to play within my area. I couldn't leave the area and others were not allowed to enter.

There was one particular person who was a lot more disrespectful than everyone else and I was disliking him more and more as the season progressed and so it was decided for the next game against this team I would come out of goal and man mark this particular player. Unfortunately during this game this player's leg got broken.

It was done in such a way that no one had seen a thing, except my brother who gave me a pat on the back as the player was carried from the pitch.

It is not something I am particularly proud of now. But it may have had something to do with renewed confidence, something I had not really experienced before.

I still didn't like to fight that much as the years of lacking confidence still remained in my head. But I was fed up of being bullied and our team was being bullied. This worm had turned.

Now as I said I didn't really like fighting but unfortunately still around this time in my life I was running around with people who had a bit of a passion for trouble. And as such I would be there or there about when confrontations occurred.

I had now started a Ska band with my school friend and there would often be trouble at our gigs as the National Front would arrive and start fights. But despite that we did quite well for a couple of years. We appeared on a compilation album with *Judge Dread* and played support to bands such as *Bad Manners, Desmond Dekker* and *The Selecter.* And we even won a couple of Battle of the Bands competitions.

There was a time when we played in Cambridge and a fight broke out between people on our minibus and some local lads. Long story short, we came off better but unfortunately we had hired a minibus from the West Kent YMCA and their name was emblazoned along the side in big letters and we were in Cambridgeshire.

Unknown to anyone the minibus had been reported to the Police. And after everyone had finished buying their fast food and had got back onto the mini bus we departed back towards Kent.

It had seemed we had gotten away with it until the van was surrounded by 3 police cars on the M11. We were told to pull over and then to turn back around at the next junction. So we were given a 3 car escort back to Cambridge I felt in my pocket and realised I still had my locking knife that I used for work to cut the boxes open.

I started thinking as we drove along they are bound to search every one of us and also the van as we entered the police compound but they never did. I did contemplate throwing it out of the window as we drove along but I was sure the police escort would have seen. Luckily for us the minibus had been reported but the person who reported the crime could not say if they saw us fighting, only that they had seen the minibus driving away and with none of the other people coming forward and with the fact that none of us talked, the Police had to let us go.

Tempting Fate

I used to have a Martial Arts patch on my flight jacket. Now this in itself was not a problem when I was in my local pub etc. but one night we decided to go to a pub that was a bit 'unsavoury'. I was not aware that it would be a problem but luckily we were with some older and wiser lads and they told me to take the jacket off to avoid any problems.

A few years later a couple of my friends and I went to support our friend who was having a bareknuckle fight with a traveller.

We were heavily outnumbered probably 10 to 1 but we stuck by our friend and after the fight we were 'invited' and I use the term loosely to join everyone in the very same pub that I had been told to take my jacket off. It turned out that it was a traveller's pub. Looking back we were probably lucky. But we never bought a drink all day.

You are immortal at '20' - aren't you?

My friends and I had been at a party and things got out of hand. Somebody had decided to start a fight with my friend. Now they thought they had the upper hand because they thought he was on his own and decided to start on him. Unfortunately for them there were actually more of us than there were of them. And they came off second best. A few of my friends got a little excited after the fight and decided to trash the house as well. As a result the Police were called.

We left the house and were walking around the streets. Whilst we were walking around somebody appeared out of a block of flats and began arguing with us. He was outnumbered 5 to 1. I think he complained we were too noisy. One of my friends went over and just hit the man, with that the man pulled a gun out. (We did wonder why he was so brave).

We all scattered. But then…and this was the really stupid part. Someone shouted it's a spud gun and we all turned around and ran back at the bloke. Now whether it was luck, fate or good timing but the Police choose that very moment to arrive with all the lights flashing. I was lucky enough to be the furthest away from the Police so never got caught although I did a nice somersault when I went flying over a tree branch in the pitch black. I was interviewed a few days later. And during the interview I asked the Police if they had seen the man with the gun. What man with a gun they asked. Again no charges were ever brought against us because the prosecution dropped the case.

The Police claimed they didn't see the man with the gun.

Film Star!!!

Guns were to feature in my life again a couple of years later. When I was in my mid-twenties my old JKD instructor, John Carrigan, was recording his own film called *The Need.*

The idea was that he could use it to further his career in acting. I had a role as one of the bad guys and I got to shoot a gun that fired blanks. There was however, a downside. I had to be shot myself.

The filming took place in a wooden shed and the idea was that John would jump down from above. I would turn around from shooting the Police out of the doorway and he would shoot, sending me flying into the wall behind me.

Looking at the wall I could see some 3x2 wooden beams, running vertically and horizontally on the wall behind me. I was thinking, I hope I don't hit one of those. Well I was about to find out as the director called "Action".

I span around. John jumped down. He shot, I flew, I missed the beams, and the Director shouted "Cut." And then he said…."Best death of the day." It was all over in one take. A star was born.

I know from John that my scene made it into the trailer for his film and it was shown to the director of *Babylon 5.* John always says that I looked before I was shot. But I maintain I didn't. I will have to watch the film again to see who was right. But if I did look you couldn't blame me. Those beams would have hurt.

How I began teaching:

For quite a few years I had been dabbling in various Martial Arts until in 1999 I found a Krav Maga school, one of only a handful in the country at the time. In Krav Maga I found something that was a lot more suited to what I was after learning. The approach to learning was more direct and a lot simpler than anything I had learned previously. And so in 2003 after attending classes for 3 years I attended and passed the IKMF Krav Maga Instructor Course.

After I passed the course it allowed me the opportunity to set up my own Krav Maga School. I hadn't really intended to teach, rather just learn the art a lot quicker. But it was my wife who encouraged me to start teaching. And so for 5 years I ran several clubs until 2008 when I got a little disillusioned with being in the EU and I was looking to take my family and move to Canada.

I decided that rather than be just a plumber, which is the job I am qualified for I would much rather teach Martial Arts full time. So I thought that I would increase my 'Saleability/ Credibility' by entering a few Martial Arts competitions and see how things went.

Martial Arts competitions were never really something I had been into, as I had a bigger interest in teaching Self Defence. But regardless I thought I would give it a go.

Competition Time!!!

I already had Black Belts in Kickboxing and Ju-Jitsu and a Brown Belt in Judo, along with various other knowledge that I had gained over the years. So I thought it may be a good chance to use the Arts I had learnt.

Around the same time one of my students was showing an interest in learning Sombo. Someone was offering a course of Sombo lessons and as I knew the Instructor running the courses I offered to go along with him. Well whilst doing the Sombo course there was a chance to enter trials to represent Great Britain in the Greek Martial Art of Pankration.

So my student and I went along for trials. Everyone was paired off with opponents according to size and weight, except me. So an open invitation was issued for someone to fight me. Just my luck. The biggest person in the room volunteered. I had seen him enter the room earlier and I thought I would not want to fight him. Well now I was.

He was younger (I was over 40), faster and nearly 20 kg heavier. He could hit hard and fast. His kicks were surprisingly quick for a big man. I was not doing too well to start with, until he went for a takedown. I quickly reversed it and got him in an arm lock. The judge's flags went up and I had won.

A few people there were picked for the team and I was one of them. As the time got nearer to go and fight in Bulgaria a lot of the fighters who were chosen began to pick up injuries. And even on the day of the flight people failed to appear and so I made the trip alone.

Things went well in the initial heats and I made it through to the final. In the final I was fighting someone from Australia. The fight started and around the 30 second mark I took a kick to the head. This was a full on kick, which is an illegal move in Pankration. It was meant to be light touch only to the head and hard contact to the body.

Whoa, the referee and the opponent seemed very distant and the voices sounded far away. The referee asked if I wanted to continue. I said yes and the fight continued. It was part of my makeup not to quit. The fight still had two and a half minutes to go and my head was swimming. But I lasted the distance and it went to the judges. I had lost but I had managed to make it to the end. My opponent said I was a tough nut to crack and I had to see the ring side doctor after to be checked over but I was a World Silver Medallist in Pankration in my first ever competition.

The following year I entered a Kick boxing competition and although I was told there would be an over 40's category it never materialised on the day. So I was offered the chance to enter the open heavy weight category for 18-40.

I had come to compete and so I took part. Things went well until I got to the semi-finals. I looked at the opponents and one of them was a very large German. I thought I hope I don't get him. But unfortunately I did. This opponent was so tall I had to stand on tiptoes and my arm went up 45 degrees just to put it around his shoulders for a photograph (I am 6 foot tall). The fight started and I kept punching and kicking. Head kicks were out due to his height. I don't really remember him doing anything much to me except walking forward every time I kicked which knocked me off balance. Again this fight went the distance and the judges couldn't separate us and so they asked us to fight for a further minute.

After the extra minute the judges decided that my opponent had won and he went into the final. I got the bronze because the other semi-finalist had his nose broken in the other semi-final.

In addition to the Kickboxing they held a Power Striking Competition. It was an open weight competition and so I thought I would have a go. Even though there were plenty of bigger fighters than myself I still managed to get a silver medal.

Due to the fact that I now had surgery on my ankle (I busted it one way playing football at West Ham Utd football club and then snapped the ligaments the other way when grading for my Brown Belt in Judo), my knees kept locking and filling with fluid (from my plumbing work) and my neck has arthritis (from a car crash), I decided that 2012 was going to be my last year for competing. I was now 43 years old and I didn't really have the enthusiasm that I had when I started competing in 2010.

Now strangely 2012 was going to be my best year for competitions. Pitted against people around my own age I came away with 4 World Championship Gold Medals in 4 different arts. I also entered the ISU Martial Arts Olympics and emerged as the Grand Champion (Champion of Champions) in the old boy's category.

Back to the development of Toxic Fighting.

In 2011 I was given my first chance to teach a seminar outside of my weekly classes. And it was in….Athens, Greece. I had to teach along with top US instructors Richard Ryan and Walt Lysak. There were also a lot of top Greek instructors there.

It was quite the baptism of fire as it was also to be filmed and released on DVD. I had also appeared in the Russell Stutely Power Black DVD set where he was trying to improve the power of various other Martial Arts Instructors, Boxers and complete novices. I believe without watching the DVD again that he said that my knee technique was 'near perfect' and that was before he showed me anything.

A couple of months later the Athens DVDs arrived in the post. It was a 3 DVD set of the seminars. After seeing these DVDs I wanted to create some of my own DVDs. One of my students knew a horror film director and so we made my first exclusive DVD.

Because this was my own DVD and contained my own techniques I decided now was a good time to adopt a name change for what I was teaching. Over the 8 years I had been teaching Krav Maga I had changed in one way or another pretty much all the techniques I had been taught and now seemed a good time to start afresh. I decided on the name Toxic Fighting System. This is because what I was teaching was not going to be beneficial to an attacker's health.

Many of the changes had come about because I often had to drive to lessons from work and I would often have a couple of hours of spare time to sit in my car and watch Martial Arts Instructional DVDs on a portable DVD player before the classes would start. That combined with my own knowledge, my students' personal knowledge and generally testing the validity of techniques I was teaching or had been taught is what made up my new Self Defence System.

I had lots of ideas and I had a class full of people who were willing to help me test and develop them. Sometimes a student would have seen a move on YouTube and they would come to class and tell me how they had seen this 'great' technique and they would proceed to show me what they had seen. Most of the time, well nearly all the time I would take the technique apart and show them why it was wrong and what they should be doing instead. And more importantly I would tell them how I arrived at my conclusion.

One of my biggest things in developing Toxic was I wanted my students to think. To have an understanding of what, why and where. After all, I would say "You need to be able to think for yourself as I won't be there when you are having a fight, unless you are fighting me".

A fight can have so many permutations that an ability to think is more important than to learn a lot of techniques.

By this time, I had developed a knack of taking a problem and turning it into a technique, even problems I never been taught or encountered before.

In some lessons, we just bought in a Martial Arts book, opened it at a random page and made a lesson up from that. Something that became apparent was that I developed a series of sayings and principles (borrowed and original). And these sayings/ principles related to how I developed Toxic. A new Toxic technique had to match my sayings/ principles. It sounds weird but this was how I filtered the validity of my techniques before they became a physical technique.

Another thing that started to happen when I was teaching seminars was that I was making up 'variations' of my techniques that I taught. This mostly occurred when I was teaching abroad as sometimes people are built slightly differently or move in a different way to how my students were taught. I had the same challenges when I was teaching people with disabilities. Sometimes teaching new people could actually help me redesign my own technique so that it was more accessible to more people.

In 2012 I made a couple more DVDs to complement the first DVD I had made. And in the second DVD one of my students who has Cerebral Palsy came along to demonstrate some of the techniques from his perspective so that people could see how simple they were and how they could be used by so many people.

In 2013 my training took another turn. I met a man called Mark Dawes. He was Ex-Navy but also a Martial Artist. But he set up a company that offered BTEC Courses in Self Defence. The first time I met him I gave him my first 3 DVDs so that he could give me his perspective on what I was teaching. And he came back with some complimentary comments.

So this is something I have done several times over now. As I am aware I do not know everything and it is always good to have some fellow martial artists I respect to give me their perspective on what I am teaching.

To date I have given copies to Don 'The Dragon' Wilson, Trevor Roberts, Cynthia Rothrock, Russell Stutely, Gary Wasniewski and Joe Carslake. And each of them have given me quotes that I have used on the back covers of my DVDs that I have recorded.

I have also given these DVDs to other much respected like Samuel Kwok, Kevin Pell, Keith Priestly, Bob Sykes and Tony Pillage to get their opinions and guidance.

In addition I later studied a lot of Mark's BTEC courses to help me understand and enhance what I was teaching and these courses included Law, Psychology, Physiology, NLP, Conflict Management and Physical Intervention. I like to think these courses helped what I have designed and made easy to learn and digest and therefore easy to recall.

I think a lot of instructors like to teach what the student wants to see. By that I mean they teach techniques that look aesthetically pleasing to the eye and that are not necessarily practical in a real life situation. I think they teach techniques like these because they think that is what the student wants.

I am not saying these techniques will not work but rather you would have to drill them extensively and also have to have the right conditions to pull them off. And often fights don't go to plan. I teach techniques born out of simplicity.

If you are in a fight and your heart is racing at 175bpm then it would be highly unlikely that those lovely rehearsed techniques learned in class are going to produce the results you expected. That is why I teach my students to think and adapt

In addition I like to think I have some different ideas with regards to Defence, Striking and Power Generation.

As an example of Power Generation, when I was training for the Pankration I was sparring with one of my students Martyn, who also did MMA. I did a hook punch to towards his ribs but instead I hit his pelvis. After that punch he called "time".

He went to the doctors the next day thinking he had torn a muscle but it turned out I had cracked his pelvis. Apparently his doctor said I must have kicked him but Martyn insisted it was a punch, we both knew it was the punch. His doctor said a punch wouldn't be powerful enough to crack a pelvic bone.

Also during the second DVD I was trying to withhold the power of my strikes during filming but I remember them saying off camera they would rather be run over by a bus than hit by me. Two of the people on the DVD had to go to hospital the next day.

I try to keep my defences simple and design my strikes to keep me as safe as possible whilst delivering a counterstrike. The power is a bonus. If you can make it work it can improve your chances of escaping much greater but it is not something we rely on too much to the detriment of other principles.

The Future…

At the time of writing this book I am travelling to the US and Europe teaching seminars and trying to get my name out there.

I seem to be quite well received in Europe, more so than in the UK. What I teach is very direct and simple and the people on the continent seem to like the approach I have to Self Defence.
Also I have been in talks about recording some more DVDs. And I would like to re-record my Fortress Defence as a package set and cover many more areas of that defence that I have not yet recorded.

I would also like to design a program so that I can roll out what I teach to as many people as I can.

And if I have the time, and if I am asked I would like to write some more for Martial Arts magazines. I have recently written quite a few articles for *Martial Arts Illustrated,* but I have also written for Martial Science and Martial Arts Guardians.

THIS IS HOW EVERYTHING CAME TOGETHER TO BECOME TOXIC.

Here at Spartan Martial Arts we are passionate about our products and services. We aim to provide the best quality equipment, at the best prices, with the best service. We offer discounts to clubs that match other well known suppliers and our care in our products is incomparable.

MADE BY MARTIAL ARTISTS FOR MARTIAL ARTISTS

www.spartanma.co.uk
info@spartanma.co.uk
01446 736682

Eddie Quinn
The Approach

Eddie Quinn is a professional martial arts teacher based in Solihull, England. He began his martial arts career in 1986. Eddie is the founder of Childsafe martial arts and The Approach Self Protection Method. He is a Muay Thai coach and lineage holder to the art of Silat Fitrah.

Eddie believes great teachers change the world for the better by helping others improve their lives, their aspirations and their outcomes.

Eddie teaches with passion, enthusiasm and an attention to detail.

In his downtime Eddie loves to travel the world and spend time with his family and two Staffordshire Bull Terriers, Buck and Lola.

How did you begin in martial arts Eddie and why?

There are four major events in my life that I am so grateful for:

meeting my wife, the birth of my two children and getting stabbed! Yes, you read it correctly, getting stabbed!

My name is Eddie Quinn and I am a UK based Martial Arts teacher.

The reason I began my martial arts journey was because of an unprovoked attack on the 23rd November 1984 when I went to the aid of three girls who were being abused by a number of youths as they were waiting for the bus.

One of the group pulled out a flick knife and stabbed me six times. I was stabbed in the right ventricle in my heart, liver, bowel, gall bladder, head and thigh. After extensive resuscitation in A&E I was handed over to a thoracic surgeon who saved my life.

During one of my outpatient appointments one of the consultants asked me if I had ever considered taking up a combat sport. I had thought about it but was yet to take any action. The doctor's words spurred me on and changed the path of my life forever.

You have to remember in those days there was no internet. There were a couple of martial arts magazines and a few books available. Even living in a big city like Birmingham martial arts clubs were still quite rare.

My best friend Steve Williams had heard about a guy who taught martial arts at a community centre about 5 miles from where I lived. We had no idea what style he taught and we didn't care! We had heard about Karate, Judo and Kung Fu but Steve and I headed down there and we watched a class. I knew from the moment I entered the Dojo that this was what I wanted to do for the rest of my life.

Which martial art was it?

It was Japanese Ju Jitsu, taught by a guy called Steve Maycock. There were around twenty people in the class and the atmosphere was electric. I can still picture that first moment when I saw people being thrown through the air, crashing down on the mat then picking themselves up and doing it all over again.I thought it was unbelievable!

How long did you train in Jiu-Jitsu?

I trained in it from 1986 to 1992. I began to read about different styles of martial arts through what channels were available at that time. I read the Bruce Lee books and the Dan Inosanto books and I became intrigued about what is now considered the norm; cross training. I wanted to be a martial artist who could be able to fight at any range.

By then I could throw and lock pretty well but I couldn't punch my way out of a paper bag! There were a few karate/kung fu clubs in Birmingham but I was intrigued about an art from Thailand called Muay Thai. I had read about how hard Thai Boxers were and how highly conditioned they were and I really wanted to learn how to hit hard.

I found a club in Birmingham that was run by Bob Spour and began to cross train in Ju Jitsu and Muay Thai. I was training 5 days a week and attended any seminar I could at weekends; obsessed wasn't the word. I began to favour Muay Thai and I fell out of love with Ju Jitsu. It was time to move on.

What was so great about the Muay Thai for you?

You get fit, learn to hit incredibly hard, you get to feel what it's like to be hit, you learn how to clinch (standing grappling) and if you want to embark on a fighting career you can do that as well. I began training in Muay Thai 26 years ago at the age of 24, now I'm 50 and I still train! It keeps my body moving, keeps me in shape and it sharpens my tools.

What art did you train in after this?

I still had this fear about knives, I knew I had to address this otherwise I would never be able to get over what had happened to me. I began to research arts that specialised in weaponry, especially knives. The South East Asian Martial arts of Silat and FMA came up in some of the books and magazine articles I read so I began to see if there were any teachers of those arts near to where I lived in Birmingham. The nearest was Martin Smith who lived in Nottingham. He taught the Latosa style of FMA I contacted him and I began to train privately with him.

As I've said I was attending every seminar I could and one guy stood out from them all, the legendary Scottish JKD instructor Rick Young. Rick is one of the most talented martial artists I have ever met, his credentials speak for themselves. I organised several seminars in Birmingham so I could learn from him.

Not only did he provide some great seminars for me - he recommended that I train with his teacher the world famous Guro Dan Inosanto. I did. It was at this seminar at Bob Breen's Academy in London that my martial arts path changed forever and led me to where I am today.

It was there I experienced the art of Pencak Silat for the first time. I was mesmerised by the fluidity of the art and of course the way Guro Dan moved. I went home, told my wife and talked her into us booking a holiday to Malaysia and Indonesia! I wanted to learn Silat.

Any luck with that?

No! I came back to the UK after a great trip to South East Asia but hadn't found anybody that taught Silat. A few weeks later I attended a Rick Young seminar that Martin Smith had organised. It was in Castle Donington, which is a 30 minute drive from my house and it was there I met my Silat Guru! I had recently purchased a video tape called 'Closing the Gap' by Chris Parker, it was advertised in Terry O Neill's *Fighting Arts International* magazine. The material looked very similar to what I had seen at Guro Dan Inosanto's seminar and I loved the way Chris transitioned from one strike to another.   As fate would have it, Chris popped along to the seminar to say hi to Rick. During a break I introduced myself and told him that I loved his video and asked if I could train with him. Chris said "Yes" and 23 years later I am still his student.

Why Silat? What's so special about it?

Chris teaches an art called Silat Fitrah. It gives me everything I need as a martial artist, from stand up fighting to ground work, Silat is a blade art that also addresses the issue of multiple attackers.

The ultimate purpose of Silat Fitrah is to develop increased self awareness, to discover who we truly are and, through that, to add value to our relationships and lives. In many ways, this is very different from The Approach Self Protection Method which is a globally recognised easy to learn method of self defence.

Tell us a little more about The Approach and how you created it.

I had been doing lots of training with a type of machete called a golok. The large circular movements I was making with the blade transitioned into really powerful hammer fist strikes and forearm strikes.

I began to experiment with my Thai Boxing class and the feedback was really positive. I showed Chris and he named these set of principles, `The Approach Self Protection Method`, and he suggested I make a DVD. Within a week I had a pilot film made. I was happy with the way I delivered the material and I filmed 3 volumes titled `The Entry System`, `Power Development` and `Multiple Strikes`.

I put an advert in *Martial Arts Illustrated* magazine and on my website and the DVDs sold all over the world! People were flying from the USA, Thailand, South Africa, The Middle East and all over Europe to attend my Instructor courses.

I was booked to teach seminars in Australia, America, Dubai, Thailand and Europe. I had always dreamt about teaching internationally and my dream had come true!

What's so good about it?

The beauty of The Approach is that it can be learned in hours, maintained in minutes and is useful forever. It has been tried and tested worldwide from military professionals, police, bodyguards and security personnel, to martial arts instructors and their students, to moms and dads and their children, The Approach really does work for everyone.

Can you elaborate?

Of course - when I say The Approach works for everyone, I really mean it.

I teach at schools and universities so I began to think of ways I could teach The Approach without relating it to blades. Whilst playing dodgeball at the end of a kids class I had a eureka moment. I realised that the forehand strike could easily be related to throwing a ball, the backhand strike to skimming a frisbee and I related the footwork to walking!

How did you begin teaching police, military etc?

I received an email from a Law Enforcement Officer in San Diego, USA. He thanked me for the prompt delivery of my DVDs. He then went on to tell me that as a defensive tactics trainer he thought The Approach was made for Law Enforcement. He then went on to say how important it is for Police, Military and Security Professionals to find a 'Hand Friendly' way of striking because they need to access their gun, baton, handcuffs etc. The Approach met all of their needs.

This was a light bulb moment for me and The Approach began to go down a different path. Over the years The Approach has been taught to members of Presidential and Prime Ministers Bodyguard Detachments, Counter Terrorist Units, Police Officers, Anti Poaching Units, and Elite Military.

How do you define martial arts and self defence, do you separate the two?

I really like what the great JKD Instructor Paul Vunak said about how he defines martial arts and self defence. He said that you should view martial arts in two categories, self perfection and self preservation. Self perfection is to learn and practice the art because you love it. Self preservation is to do whatever it takes to stay alive and get home to your loved ones.

Growing up in Birmingham in the late 70's and early 80's I knew all about self preservation. I have been on the receiving end of violence on more than one occasion and I know what its like to get bludgeoned, stabbed and attacked by multiple attackers. If you practice a martial sport you only have to worry about one opponent, there are rules and a referee. In a self defence situation you do not have that luxury and the threat of multiple opponents and weapons is very possible. Rick Young sums it up perfectly, he said to me many years ago that we must know the reasons why we train.

What does the future entail?

I am just about to launch my first Online Training Pack in The Approach Self Protection Method that I am really excited about. It is a series of compact lessons where you can watch from your phone, tablet or laptop and train along with me.

I have a new website www.eddiequinnmartialartsteacher.com where I shall be sharing my thoughts and observations in my Blog.

I shudder to think what my fate would have been If I didn't take the advice of my heart specialist 30 years ago and take up a martial art. My martial arts teachers helped me to rebuild my life and that is the reason I became a teacher. I am living proof that martial arts can be used as a vehicle to change your life.

I hope that through my Blog, online training and seminars I can continue to teach and inspire lots more people around the world.

What do you think makes a great teacher?

Wow Dan that answer could take up several volumes! I will tell you which one I think is perhaps the most relevant to martial arts. I strongly believe that the teacher should be the best student in the room because learning never stops.

Final question Eddie. What would you say to the guy who stabbed you if you saw him today?

I would shake his hand and say thank you!

I can honestly say that I feel no hate or animosity towards him. If it wasn't for getting stabbed I would never have gone down this magical road of being a martial artist. I wouldn't have helped people change their lives, I wouldn't have instilled confidence in the thousands of children I have taught and I wouldn't have travelled all over the world training and teaching.

Like I said at the start of this interview, getting stabbed is one of the events in my life that I am truly grateful for.

The journey continues.

Contact details:

Email: theeddiequinnapproach@gmail.com

Website: www.the-approach.com

Blog: www.eddiequinnmartialartsteacher.com

The Tri-Brand Alliance
Phil Norman, Bob Breen and Andy Norman

This section introduces the martial arts tri-brand of Defence Lab, 4D Combat and Ghost. Andy, Phil and Bob have known each other for years on the Jeet Kune Do circuit and although they each have their own unique spin on their arts, they collaborate and work together. As we will hear, each style is not that dissimilar from the others, and in the martial arts world where people are quick to bad mouth other styles, it's a refreshing change to see high calibre martial artists working together for the good of the industry as a whole.

Phil Norman
Ghost Elusive Combat

Phil Norman is a Jeet Kune Do and Kali legend and the main man behind the Ghost Elusive Fighting System that is taking the world by storm. A direct student of Dan Inosanto, Phil has competed in MMA and appeared on the *Gladiators* TV show and is now making waves in the martial arts world through Ghost. Here we talk to Phil about his history and the development of Ghost and where it will go in the future.

When did you begin martial arts and why? How did you feel walking into your first class?

I was 17 when I started training in traditional Kung Fu and with Luck Crane under Master They. It was there I met Colin Sherred, who became a good friend and training partner, along with Steve

Mosely we became the seniors at the club and trained daily in and out of the club.

Tell us about how you became involved with JKD, Kali etc. with Guro Dan Inosanto, what is he like?

Guro Dan Inosanto has been the most inspirational person in my life, a genuinely beautiful person who has given so much to not only the martial arts world but also increased exposure to the many cultures from where it came.

At 18, I attended a 4 day training seminar with my training partner Colin Sherred, led by Guru Dan Inosanto in London at Nino Bernardo's Basement Gym. It was a 'life changing' experience. Immediately we asked where we could train JKD, Kali? And Guro said 'you should come over to the Academy' ....so we did! We also attended his seminars in the UK and Europe and then we made regular visits to the Inosanto Academy in California.

Whilst I was there I took all the classes and in 1989 I became the first UK based student to pass Ajarn Surachai Sirisute's Thai test and also received his Initiateur (Instructor) in Boxe Francais Savate under Professeur Salem Assli. In 1991 Phil became an apprentice instructor under Guru Dan Inosanto in the Filipino Martial Arts Kali/ Silat and in Jun Fan Martial Arts/Jeet Kune Do.

Talk to us a little about your time on *Gladiators*

I did *Gladiators* for a laugh…but at the same time trained seriously. I did my research, worked out what specific physical attributes needed training and did it. My martial arts training prepared me mentally for the shows and I believe that was what took me through. I went up against faster, stronger and more agile contestants, but I am convinced that I was stronger mentally and had a more positive psychological approach that was needed to handle the pressure of this event. I witnessed this with other contestants who were martial artists. I went onto to win the season and represented the UK in the international programmes in the USA and in South Africa. It was from these TV shows that I picked up the fight name 'The Gladiator', a title I was never quite able to shake off.

Talk about your career in the ring and cage

With most of my instructors being based in the USA, it was difficult to get quality instruction for personal training locally. This led me to start training with a close friend who I had met through security work, namely Trevor Ambrose, a World Champion kick boxer (later winning 4 other World Title Belts!). I trained with Trevor privately almost on a daily basis and went with him to compete in France at a Kick Boxing event (we both won, Trevor by KO, myself by stoppage).

It was shortly after this, that I suffered a severely prolapsed disc and the doctor told me that I would never be able to do martial arts again! I was laid up for 6 months and struggled to come to terms with the injury. I realized I could not rely on my body to make an income, so I took pain killers and went to University and studied sport science.

During this time I started to make a remarkable recovery and went back to training, at first very gently with specific back exercises, but it was not long before I was back training in the martial arts. It was at that time that I started training in Judo with Dave Kavanagh, a 5th Dan, who was coaching the British Sport Ju Jitsu Team in grappling and throwing. At the time the team included the likes of K1 Champion Gary Turner, Alex Reid and Buster Reeves. I was invited to join the team for a training weekend and subsequently asked to represent Great Britain in World Championships. In 1998, 2 years after being told I would never be able to compete in martial arts again, I won the middle weight Sport Ju Jitsu World Title, beating fighters from Japan, Canada and the USA.

I continued to compete and fought on one of the early Mixed Martial Art shows held in the UK, 'Night of the Samurai', winning by KO and becoming the British Champion. In 2000 I took and passed the Shooto exam under Sensei Yorinaga Nakamura and became the first UK student to get a 100% pass rate. In the same year, I became one of only 5 Students in the UK to be awarded the honour of his Full Instructorship under Guru Dan Inosanto.

I completed my University studies passing with honours and changed from door work to lecturing at a local college in order to develop my teaching skills.

I still competed but it was getting more difficult at work as early MMA was getting bad press so I would fight every now and then.

At the age of 40 I fought one last time in MMA, breaking my hand and foot, securing a points win regardless after which I decided my body had had enough abuse and retired from competition. This led to a time of reflection and the 'bringing together' of the elusive fighting system I have named Ghost™ elusive combat

The development of Ghost

The name Ghost was inspired by my old training partner Trevor Ambrose. I have often said how our first sparring session was like getting beaten up by 3 guys whilst trying to hit a Ghost. His movement seemed often disjointed and unorthodox so much that he was difficult to hit. This had occurred naturally and I wanted to try and replicate it. Trevor schooled me in the art of ring craft but it wasn't until I was watching one of my other instructors Sifu Rick Faye at a seminar that I saw a link with the weapons based system Kali. The shape I saw Sifu Rick Faye make when he was avoiding a stick was similar to the one I saw Trev make when he avoided a punch. This led into me trying to find links with Kali at first and then progressed into shapes and techniques that became more appropriate for the sport model. I tried to start working it in classes but a lot of experienced students were not so keen as they had to sacrifice power for movement initially. I continued researching it for the next few years knowing that I was onto something but disappointed that some of the senior students were not embracing this new method (The name Ghost came later). Then along came Jake Clarke.

He was a junior who had been training in my classes from the age of 10, at 15 he took his black belt which was being assessed by Trevor. Afterwards he came to me and said what's next? I was getting frustrated with my older students not seeing what I was seeing in the elusive style I was working and so I thought OK let's try it with you! The thing about Jake is that he was not naturally very fast or strong in fact he was quite small for his age and he lived 14 miles away from his nearest class. But he was committed and very passionate about learning and so it began, and the style Ghost Elusive Combat took off.

Within 6 months Jake was running rings around all the seniors in sparring and another new student showed commitment and loyalty and his name was Xavier Sedras. Again another youngster who with a little training started to also get a lot of success with the seniors. The next stage was to see how it held up in competition as being a sport martial art it could be tested. Over the next few years the Ghosters competed regularly winning titles whilst also adjusting and adapting the Ghost to each new challenge and they have been essential in helping me develop what is today recognized globally as Ghost - an elusive combat system designed for sport fighting where the rules allow to stand and strike!

How did you become involved with the tri-brand of DL?

The Tri Brand was the brain child of Defence Lab creator Andy Norman. My research for Ghost also took me to look at Defence Lab or Keysi as it was termed then as an option for dealing with those who would try and counter long range Ghost with a clinch.

For us the area the DL students fight in was one we as Ghosters would try and stay out of, but we did have opponents try to move in for the clinch a lot more as they tried to counter Ghost. I had the opportunity to catch up with Andy at a seminar we were both teaching on held by Eddie Quinn, and we got on really well. Andy had gone through the similar ridicule I had with Ghost and encouraged me to keep chasing what I was doing. He offered his support which I immediately accepted as I had witnessed the empire he had built with Keysi and then again with Defence Lab. Having practically no business / marketing training I was very pleased to get his input. This led to the idea of working together and with Guro Bob Breen also coming in the Tri Brand was formed.

What are your current thoughts on the state of martial arts in the UK and abroad?

I think the martial arts in the UK in some areas are as good as any other country, but unfortunately I think it's also stagnated in others. The exposure through internet and access to training online means now it is so much easier to train and get high level tuition. I think some of our sport fighters are doing exceptionally well on the world stage. But I also think there are a lot of people/instructors who are stuck in their comfort zones. From a recreational perspective I think this is not a bad thing we are having more participate in martial arts than ever before and benefiting from better health. It's better that they train in a comfort zone than to lose them to another sport or computer games.

Plans for Jake and X?

Jake and X are still very heavily helping me with my research and development of Ghost and I still have big plans for the pair of them. Jake has just made the switch from Kick Boxing into Amateur Boxing because of health reasons (diagnosed Celiac which led to type 1 diabetes) and I want to avoid unnecessary damage to his legs. He has just made the England squad at elite level so pushing him into international competition with an Olympic dream. Xavier on the other hand is making waves in the MMA scene so if we can keep him injury free we should see him on the world stage in the not too distant future

Plans for the future of Ghost?

Keep doing what we are doing we are hooked up nicely with the Tri Brand so it is important to maintain its honesty and integrity in its future development. The next main goal is to increase its exposure globally and so a lot of work is being done to achieve this through online training.

Bob Breen
4D Combat

Guro Bob Breen is quite simply a legend in the martial arts world. One of Dan Inosanto's inner circle, he is often called the Godfather of JKD in Europe and in total has introduced 7 different styles of martial arts to Europe. His 4D system is making waves in the martial arts world for total stand up combat and he has worked on films such as *Deadpool* and TV hits like *The Walking Dead*.

Tell us about how you became involved in martial arts then. Why did you start and how did you feel walking in to your first class?

It was that time when Karate was happening in the early 60s.

People were hitting things with Karate chops and claiming to be the hardest man in the world but nobody knew anything! Up until then it was just boxing, judo and fencing. However I saw a little bit of stuff on TV, and at the same time a friend at school said to me that he was doing Karate too. So I asked where he was training and he was at the YMCA so I went along and had a look to see what it was all about. Tatsuo Suzuki was teaching and I remember thinking that I'd never seen anybody move so fast in my life! I'd had lots of fights and what I'd noticed in all the fights I'd had was it would be great to have some technique and I had none!

I didn't really like the boxing training back then, Amateur boxing back then wasn't based on technique, generally they'd just stick you in the ring with a good chance you'd come out with a broken nose and if you came back the week after they'd teach you a little bit. It was pretty brutal and I thought it was just a bit stupid. But I saw the Karate and was hooked instantly. I loved the training with Tatsuo. I remember in my first sparring class I went into a big deep stance and got kicked straight in the groin! So I thought to myself, okay that doesn't work so I changed that! It was a great time though and within around 3 years it changed my whole life. I was obsessed by the time I was 17 and obsessed about getting my green belt. My other friends were going out and getting into trouble, so that was really a parting of the ways. Instead of going out I trained to do my green belt and that was kind of it for me! They went one way and I went another way. How lucky was I?

As I said, I was obsessed and I wanted to get in the sparring team but that was for black and brown belts only. But I argued my case and said that I really wanted to fight! One night we had a competition a team thing and they didn't have enough people so they said for me to join in and that was it, I was in the team. One of my first fights, the girlfriend of the guy I was fighting knew me from the old groups I used to hang around with and was screaming at him to kill me! He obviously didn't but it was really funny. I trained hard then got my black belt when I was 20 and, now looking back I suppose I was incredibly arrogant or just single minded, as I opened a school! I was one of the first people in England who wasn't Japanese to open a school. It was a Japanese only thing up until then, very hierarchical. I was one of the first English Black belts so I opened a school at 20 and that was it, I was off! Teaching and training.

How was the teaching for you? Was it a steep learning curve?

It was just about the love for me so I got 5 students, then 10 students then 20 maybe. It wasn't like it is now with online marketing and businesses. It was putting up a sign and then just seeing who turned up! But I held on to these people for years, some of whom I know even now! Terry Barnett, who is a great guy and very close friend, started training with me when he was 12, told me he was 14, but he was 12 and now he's an incredible martial artist and life-long friend. I was doing a lot of competition back then and enjoyed that, it was different to how it is now. It was very amateurish, we'd just go to the competitions and fight. It wasn't a thing we were training for specifically, we were just always training but it wasn't as athletic as it is now, so in that way it was more like a real fight.

I think the athleticism today is much better. We all worked out, but sometimes we'd also go to the pub beforehand then compete so it was more like a fist fight you'd have in a way. There were no pads so a few teeth got lost, it was fairly intense at times. Now athletically, it's much better, but in terms of grit and hardness, some of the people that came out of that era are legends – Terry O'Neill, Gary Spiers, really tough men that people are still talking about. I remember at the British Team training there was one guy who was a Rugby League player, Ron Wade I think his name was, and he gave Gary Spiers a back kick full on, he was a big guy and Spiers just laughed it off and went "ha, good kick"! That's when you think woaahhh!

I then went to Japan in 1974 and trained at the Nichi-Dai which was the home of Wado-Ryu Karate and that's where they trained their teams, one of the best clubs in Japan. It was all about competition so we went there and the training was incredibly hard, we'd run barefoot up to shrines over the gravel and stuff so it was tough! I came back and fought for England again as I had previously. This time I was team captain against the Japanese and we beat them. So that was a game changer. It was a weird time and things were changing and people were starting to look at cross-training.

There was a book out called *Modesty Blaise* and the author of that in 1963 was talking about timing, beats and mixing fencing with punches and cross-training stuff. Basically being renegade! He did a few novels the best of which was *Sabre Tooth* so the idea of being non-conformist was already out there and by the time Bruce came along we were all primed for it. Bruce obviously pushed it massively, but the idea was already there through *Modesty Blaise.* Bruce came along late 60s early 70s but we were already kind of doing it!

In my own club we were doing boxing, judo and karate as I was always exploring. Then I'd say to people let's get down on the ground and they'd whinge their suit would get dirty but hey who cares! It was a new idea to do that as usually people just looked at the stand up. Were we great at it? No probably not, and we only had bits of pieces. Bruce Lee came along and he was genius and integrated it all, not perfectly, but he integrated it and he was a huge inspiration.

Did that change things?

I was into that whole idea of JKD and so contacted Dan Inosanto and heard nothing for years! But I did get into Escrima, It's a bit of a convoluted story but I had been teaching Jeff Roth privately, he was the guy who founded *Combat* magazine. We were driving one day and reading another martial arts magazine which was more of a cultural thing rather than a thing about fighting so I said that it needed more combat! Two weeks later he came back and showed me the banner heading, so he was a bit like you in that he just had an idea then went out and did it! He asked if I wanted to be on the front cover of the first magazine so we did the photoshoot and everything, then this guy called Bruce Lee came along and supplanted me as the leading man! I had a big article on the inside of the magazine in around 1974 as I had just come back from Japan. Soon after that a telephone engineer came to my house and he recognised me from *Combat* and said "I'm Jay Dobrin. I train Escrima" I was intrigued by that so did it with my friend, Ralph Jones, for about a year with Jay and people like Bill Newman, Brian Jones, there were around 6 of us that I trained with that was it.

I then heard from Dan who said he was over the week after so would I like to organize something? I said sure, so from my own school I got 50 people then a few odds and ends as well and we had the first Dan Inosanto seminar in England! It was fantastic, he came with Jeff Imada who arranged the fight scenes for all the *Bourne Identity* films! On that first evening it was Dan and Jeff and it was incredible! We looked at sticks, knives, everything, no breaks, just a tour de force and I knew that's what I wanted to do!

I then changed my school. I had classes of 40+ people and I changed everything overnight and we went down to 8. But I would never change back, I was on that track and there was no going back. Some liked the rigid stances of Karate so they left and others had their reasons, but like I said, it was my track and I had to go on it. It was like jazz and classical music and they couldn't understand the jazz just then. Everyone is doing jazz now and they understand as it's evolved but back then people couldn't see it as it didn't have exclamation marks and full stops like Karate did. I just changed and that was it and I've been on that track ever since!

You became one of Dan's inner circle, how did that come about?

I just said yes! He asked if I wanted to come, I was there. I just said yes when others might say no! Even if he didn't ask I'd turn up! It was a great time, an adventure and I met fabulous and interesting people. Dan is very inclusive and so if he's going training with someone like Rigan Machado or Edgar Sulite he'll say for me or others to come along! We could train with Machado, famous yoga teachers, all these fabulous people who are the best of the best, doing everything from gyro tonics to BJJ! It was just an incredible time! We were training and learning all day, it was knackering, and I was mentally full! All these people individually are just huge and a well you can drink from for years and Dan's doing this every day! We all try to keep up, Erik Paulson, Rick Young, myself and we can't do it! We do about half a day and we're mentally done! He was so open and introduced me to so many people and I just said yes! Simple as that really.

Through Dan's introductions I trained in New York living in the Bronx, travelled the world training and learning from the best in knife, blade etc. All because of Dan. I had great friends and we'd do all sorts; like attacking people in the shower Kato style, it was mad but it was great. I introduced a lot of people to Europe, but also went various places such as the Philippines for the first World Masters Convention in 1987 so I went on that and again, it was great. Lots of different styles, lots of different people.

We then formed WEKAF (World Escrima, Kali, Arnis Federation) as we wanted to spread it more around the world so we said let's do it! I think there were six of us around the table from various nationalities and so we just formed WEKAF. That then became the host of the first World Escrima Championships which was in 1989.

I took a team to the Philippines and fought along with a few other great guys who were all beasts! In 1992 we took another team back and they really went for it and got a few World Champions out of that. It was a fabulous time but I was introducing all these people to Europe, so I think all in all we've introduced 7 different styles into Europe that people hadn't heard of.

Where did you then go from there then, did you need a new challenge?

I think at this point I was already starting to form the 4D Combat even though I didn't realise it yet. We bought the first BJJ black belt in so I was training some ground work, and I was also training this short guy from Hull called Andy Norman that some people have heard of! I was just on that path of doing stuff and having a good club. At that time The Academy was one of the best clubs in Europe. A really tough but very friendly club.

I'd heard that. What do you think made it special? Did that lead to you wearing your hips out?

Well the Academy in Hoxton was formed in about '88, we'd always trained hard so that attracted a certain type of person. The club was a unique place, a mix of martial artists, girls doing aerobics and a gay group who used the gym facilities. Surprisingly it worked amazingly well. The martial arts guys were all very passionate about being better so we were just pushing it on all fronts. For instance, from around 1980 we'd added the Karrimor Mountain Marathon into the mix. It's a two day fell run in the Lake District and to pass black belt in my academy you had to do that. So I was doing lots of endurance events and over 200 miles on the bike a week among other things. So I was leading from the front. By the time we'd opened the club that vibe just continued. However, as a result of that I wore my hips out plus I was eating drinking and enjoying life to the full, shall we say! I got some health problems with my gut and then I'd also worn my hips out. So from 36 years old to around 50 years old it was pretty tough! In 1989 I fought in the first World Stick Fighting Championships, but by 1992 I could fight still, but not well enough to be in the team so I was the coach. It got to the

MARTIAL MASTERS Vol 1

point where I could barely walk so I started to develop along 4D lines from then.

So how did you fight people and even keep up with them, but not be able to move well?

I realised I could walk slowly in and out and I could find the space within space. I knew where I was and how not to get hit, how to put little roadblocks in their way. That was the beginning of 4D. I realised I needed to manipulate them and play with their time and not be on the end of their time. We'd do silly things like all the knife defence, but with our feet in a laundry box so we couldn't move around as much. What would you do without your feet? That was my party trick. Try and stab me while I'm stood in a laundry box! So I developed lots of the things that you now see.

I had my hips replaced in 2001, but I had 15 years of trying to figure out how to move as efficiently as possible and I investigated walking! How do I walk in invisible, hit you and walk out? As it's normal, you don't see me, then SMASH, and I'm out again, it was just good timing and I was getting really good guys! You walk in, hit, walk out. They just miss you each time and you enter in again and people go what the hell are you doing!! I found the space within the space. So in 2001 when the hips were replaced I'd had 15 years of testing and figuring this stuff out. Then I added the rest of the stuff on. When we were talking earlier, I was thinking what was I doing those years, and I now realise those were my years of experimenting, teaching, going head to head with people, but my legs weren't really working so it was a great experience in a way.

Great experience?

Most people wouldn't think of it like that, but then all the Breen's are ridiculously optimistic! They'd say things like 'Oh a tidal wave, what a lovely way to get to the beach earlier!' It's a family curse. So you have to find the positive, no dark clouds for us! Coming to

210

terms with it and the club was tricky, but it made me look at what I was doing and that was really the beginning of 4D and what we've developed now to take out to the world.

You've had thousands of students over the years - were any of them special?

I have many but a few stand out. Terry Barnett, David Onuma, Neil Mcleod, Andy Norman, Simon Wells, Winston Fraser, Gordon McAdam, Alex Turnbull to name only some of them from that era. I'm still good friends with all of them. For instance, my relationship with Andy Norman is like that with Terry Barnett - long lasting. We've always kept in touch. He was one of those exceptional students who commit totally. He'd travel to London from Hull every week for a private lesson, sometimes twice in a week. Over time he'd become a close friend. About that time I took Andy and David Onuma to America to teach a seminar with 300 black belts so we went and taught there which was a big old eye opener for us! 300 black belts! There were 300, but they weren't black belts of the standard I would have given but hey, still 300 black belts!

So how did Andy get into KFM?

Andy went to Spain with me after this for a seminar and he whinged he didn't like Spain so I basically told him to shut up and enjoy it. He had a great time as it wasn't the tourist Spain it was Sagunto! There I introduced him to Justo Diegez who was also a student of mine in Spain, so whatever happened I guess that's my fault! It's all gone through me. Both of those guys were exceptional because they always said yes to life! He met Justo there and they got on straight away so became firm brothers and were then doing JKD under me. They then evolved that into the KFM and obviously now Andy has Defence Lab so I'm really happy as I was a part of that and without me it probably wouldn't happen. I think I inspired them to think differently. Often whilst teaching Andy in those early days I'd get him to question everything; why would he do a complex thing if I could still hit him. It was teaching him to think and if I've done anything over the years it's teaching people how to think strategically. To spread that type of thinking, that's my thing I think! How do I beat you without having to work hard!

What happened then?

They went off and did the films such as *Batman* and I plugged on doing what I was doing travelling all over the world teaching JKD but with a very Breen blend as I never really fitted into the JKD mould. I was always the heretic, with people saying what I was doing wasn't JKD and you realised they were just as stuck in the classical mess as Bruce was talking about, they were just turning Bruce's art into that. There was that split in the nucleus of JKD, Dan was the heretic for the nucleus and I was the heretic way off, I was Dan's naughty child!

I did those JKD and Kali videos in 1992 and I still get people coming up to me saying they loved them and are still watching them now! For them it changed their whole opening and way they saw martial arts and so that's a lovely thing to hear. Jackie Chan's bodyguard apparently even loves it and raves about it so that's a pretty cool thing to hear and get that sort of feedback from people who understand things.

So how did you and Andy get back together again?

I met Andy a few years ago in Italy. We'd always had a close bond and just thought we should do something together as we were both asking questions that should be asked, and answering them. It's the same with Phil Norman who is another innovator; we'd fallen out with each other for some reason 30 years ago over something silly that neither of us remember! I met Phil again and went down to his club and taught a seminar and we just hit it off again. He and I are on the phone together every day now talking concepts and so we're back on! All three of us went, hang on we're all doing the same stuff, but expressing it differently. The concepts are the same stuff however more or less! We're all getting off the angle and it's basically JKD but on steroids! I think Bruce Lee would be very pleased with what we've done.

So is this a new JKD?

It depends on your viewpoint. It's one evolution of a unique approach. Others are staying where they are and are copying - however for me the thing I loved about JKD was stripping away, not adding. I've now seen people doing complex JKD drills and I just think no, that's not it, what's the concept? It's been great for all of us because we inspire each other every day. We talk to each other all the time and gain inspiration from each other. Of course we all nick stuff from each other, then run with it and extrapolate. However our arts all look totally different from each other.

Do the students like it?

I think what's really good for me is that 4D has had a huge impact on the club. It's got bigger as it's got more structure. Everything is based around one thing and so it's easier to understand. I'm teaching a lot of professional guys with around 20-40 years of training and even they're going wow! I get it! It all fits together! We teach them to hit harder than they've ever hit before, guys that have been on the doors for 20+ years or pro MMA athletes and they love it! It's a joyous thing and I get paid for it! I also hang around with great people like Matt Chapman, James Evans-Nichol and Tony Davis, they teach me lots of things about martial arts as a business and they're just fabulous people. On top of that I'm still really tight with my most senior student David Onuma. Then I've got the 4D team guys too. All smart people. I've got a great team around me it's just perfect!

Martial arts are famous for being very political what do you think to all this and the state of martial arts?

I have great students and friends who are all doing their own thing. It doesn't mean I can't work with them or be friends with them just because I'm doing something a little different. I think we're doing virtuous work and if you get paid it's even better.

What about the future in martial arts?

I think there are a lot of followers in the martial arts now. I play jazz, very badly, but a little bit and when I was in a band someone asked me who I was following. I said the bass, but he said the bass was following the drums, who was following me so we're all going down together. You need to have your own rhythm and do your own thing and that's something Jason Rebello, who used to play piano for Sting told me. Have your own thing and don't anchor on anyone else.

I see lots of people on YouTube with fancy pattern drills chasing hands all over the place but they're all following. There's very little original stuff out there. Tyson doesn't do lots of fancy pad drills, he just bangs hard and smashes his opponents with good skills and mechanics, not I hit your hands with my pads, it's rubbish! There's lots of nonsense out there that's pretty and shiny, but it's rubbish, but unfortunately attractive. Having developed 4D I can ignore most of the nonsense parts of YouTube and concentrate on a few good examples. I like looking at Floyd Mayweather and the good Thai fighters like Samart, but for stand up there's not a lot out there with a good skill level. We're just aiming to make 4D intelligent combat and using the JKD thing of simple, direct and effective.

Where did 4D combat in its present form come from and how did it develop?

I needed to put down in concrete form what I was doing and what I'd learned over the years. I'm 66 now and thought how do I define what I'm doing? What am I good at that will help people master martial arts?

I thought I'm really strong at striking, clinching, weapons and group attack, that's a huge area let's just deal with that. We said yes to that and those techniques, but also no to techniques where you could possibly end on the ground.

I'm not bad on the ground and was one of the original guys doing groundwork in England, but it's not my speciality so why would I teach people badly when they can do and train with an expert? Strategically I still remember vividly if you go to the ground you get kicked.

Similarly in 4D we don't really do too many kicks as with adrenaline going, you can easily end on the ground. We wanted a strategy to deal with stand-up fighting and so we came up with the concept of the map which is on all our t-shirts. It mapped out a fight, here's the attack, here's the possible defences, the possible counter-strikes etc. Almost a blueprint for an attack! That applies for weapons too as well as clinch and group attack so we think it's pretty cool!

So it's a sort of one plan to control everything?

In a way yes. The things we train happen all the time, so our percentages go way up! Because I know what's next in order of play due to the map, I know where I am and I know what your choices are so I can respond to them at all times. I then limit your choices, you might come to the table with 4, but I limit them to 2 or 1. If you only have one choice, I can just wait then, I know my response. Whoever you are, and whatever range you're at, you only have two arms, two legs and a head so I know exactly where you are on the map. I drill all the head drills for example, you throw your head in and I say thank you! It's almost like playing the blues; you know what chord you play and which chord comes next. Once you understand that you can do anything. It's simple, but super deep! I can get everything from finger locks, to head locks, to punching, to back clinching, there's no thought there I just react. I don't look for anything; you just give it to me! I've got some guys who teach the special groups in the police and for them it's perfect as it's all about force escalation. With the 4D it's very CCTV aware. I don't really want to fight, oops I got you in the eye, I don't want to fight but here's an elbow, please stop oh there's a spear hand. It looks very passive, but when you're on the other end of it, you're getting done all the time, eyes, throat, groin, chin and I hit very hard structurally. When I hit you, I hit you with the planet! Matt Chapman always says to me he hates my punches as they're just so nasty! I'm not bigging myself up but you can teach anyone that, once you hit them with the planet, they don't get up because it's structurally right. There's a kind of beauty in it. You're an egg and here's an anvil. Boom!

You recently worked on *Deadpool*, how did that come about?

Deadpool was predominantly through Andy, although I've done a few other things like *The Walking Dead*, they wanted us to do something with their stunt team and they thought I was the best person to go to. They're in Atlanta so it's nice to hear from that far away that your stuff is being recognised. But for *Deadpool* I worked with Ed Skrein who's a fantastic guy and a fantastic athlete. He's the real deal and has his feet on the ground. He's very handsome so I never get photos taken with him! He's very easy to teach and understands it! We helped him a bit for *Deadpool* and had to make some of the moves a bit bigger for the movie but it's good stuff with the axes and stuff where you can see he's an athlete. We're hoping to do more with him in the future so I think he's currently watching our training pack number 1 which is out now!

What's the future for 4D then?

The online training is now out and the first pack is available. It's a bit of a taster and just says this is the 4D concept. The website is 4dcombat.com and you can buy it on there. We're also building an instructor group as well so have instructor camps regularly. We're just trying to spread it very organically as we want it to be good! It's based on high quality training so it's not for everyone, but it's for people that understand. It's good! We're working very closely with Andy and Phil so we'll see how that goes but it's going great at the moment! So that's it really, we have lots of people asking us to go out and teach in Asia, Japan, Thailand etc. to spread it that way. I think we're going to go slow and get it right, and just make sure it's good, but it's nice stuff and feels lovely as it's true, there's no bullshit in it.

How do you mean?

A big thing in 4D is to learn something and then test it. Can you hit me? So you try and hit each other, lightly of course. Oh you can't well good! For instance if I'm going to try and attack you as soon as you see me move, don't let me. That way you just get better. We test everything and make sure it works. The essence is on people to learn it first, then try to break it or counter it and see what the weaknesses are. That's the ethos, we test everything. For instance I can hit you with my jab 8 out of 10 times in the face and you can't stop me and that's when I've told you what I'm going to do and I still get 8 out of 10. Test it and you can trust it.

It sounds fantastic.

It's nice, lots of the seasoned guys are loving it. It's good for beginners and for very advanced guys too. Based on simple things that are instinctive to do. The sort of things that everyone does. What's unique is you do less as they do more. It's very strategic, you've got a plan and a map so in many ways you're ahead.

Importantly it's fun to train yet very functional. As deep as you want yet easy to learn and teach.

Andy Norman
Defence Lab

Andy Norman is the driving force behind the global phenomenon that is Defence Lab. From his roots in Karate, through to Jeet Kune Do with Bob Breen, and finally his development of KFM and subsequently Defence Lab, he has certainly led an interesting life. His big break came when he was asked to work on the blockbuster hit *Batman Begins* and subsequently other Hollywood hits such as *Jack Reacher* and *Mission Impossible III*. Andy talks to us about his development of Defence Lab, his own martial arts roots and what the future holds.

Let's start with you at the beginning, why did you start martial arts and when?

My earliest memory, which is a strange one, is of a program called *The Avengers*. I remember watching two guys in it chasing the lead character, whilst in the middle of a fight the two bad guys punched the corners of these walls and punched straight through them. I think I was around 8 or 9 at the time and just went, `I want to do that`! So it wasn't a Bruce Lee thing at the time that got me into martial arts, it was *The Avengers*. I searched the local karate club out, and that was to be the beginning of my martial art journey. So, it was a TV program and someone punching straight through a wall that fuelled my inquisitive little brain! I went to the local Karate centre with a friend, needless to say as a child I was nervous, but at the same time I was super curious. Due to the fact that I was only 9 years old I was totally blown away by the whole ethos of martial arts and I was highly inspired. I trained in Wado Ryu Karate from 9 to around 18 and by the time I was 18, like all people, I thought I was Bruce Lee.

An event that changed my destiny

When I was 18 years old, and whilst walking home from the city one night, I managed, via ego, to get myself into a rather eventful fight with 5 guys. I was walking past these lads sat on a wall with a friend of mine, one of whom was 6ft plus and a big old bruiser. One of these lads threw an empty bag of chips still laced with vinegar at us and the vinegar went all over my mate. Me being of small stature, hence carrying the classic small man syndrome, and generally just having an anarchic character turned round straight away and went "fucking come on then"! They all stood up, and me thinking I was Bruce Lee and having a 6ft plus friend with me, well, I was up for it, only when I turned to my friend in order to check he was primed and ready, all I saw was him running in the opposite direction as fast as possible, great I thought, thanks, by the time I turned back round I'm was in the middle of a chaotic fight with 5 guys.

Bish bosh bash! I did 3 of them, hurt the 4th one and ran from the 5th one. A couple of hundred metres down the road, I'm starting to calm down a little bit but I'm shaking and can't close my hand as it's broken. I was probably around half a mile from home, and during that half mile walk home I had an absolute brain meltdown. I started thinking intensely, my mind was spinning; I've been training all these years and nothing in there worked. The only thing that saved me was instinct. Grabbing them, nutting them, spitting at them and punching. All the techniques I had trained over the years simply hadn't worked for me! It's not to say that any specific art doesn't work, it was simply the things I had personally trained didn't express themselves as I thought they should when the moment called upon them. The whole experience simply melted my brain and made me question everything. As many young lads, I'd been scrapping throughout my school days, but this was the first proper fight I'd had where I'd really felt the reality and true dangers of a street fight. It was a very real, and very serious moment in life, and one that could have got me in a very serious mess. That was to be the night I quit martial arts. I'd spent X amount of years training 2-3 times a week yet nothing came out, I'd been training so hard and had an incredible love for the martial arts, but that one event changed my entire world, and my perception and blunt reality of the fighting arts.

It was around 3 years later; I saw an advert for Bob Breen in London, connected to Bruce Lee and Dan Inosanto. I knew a little about Dan Inosanto, but didn't really understand the Kali and Jeet Kune Do world in the UK and Europe. I rang the Academy in

Hoxton, London and made an appointment for a private lesson with Bob Breen, and thought I'll just go down and check this thing out. That visit to London and that first private lesson with Bob Breen re-ignited my passion for the fighting arts. Bob Breen set me on the path that really changed everything for me, the way I thought and felt, so I consider Bob Breen as the true beginning of my martial arts experience.

I travelled down to London from Hull every week sometimes twice a week for private lessons. I did that for many, many years. At that time, I was spending between £200 and £250 a week. That would include petrol to the train station, the train to London, food, underground and my lessons with Bob. I did that for probably just shy of a decade so it was a massive investment for me. When Bob was travelling I would ask if I could go with him, and after a certain amount of time he obviously felt I was at an assistant kind of level in terms of what he required from me. I travelled the world with him and had some great adventures.

Let's talk about the KFM then, when did you first meet Justo?

I first met Justo when I went on my travels with Bob Breen to teach a seminar at Justo's academy. Bob and myself taught the seminar and afterwards, Justo and I did a little more training, we ended up having a roll around and discussed, in our very limited communication skills, about our personal direction with regards to combat studies and the methodologies that supported our thoughts. There was definitely a spark there, I wasn't quite sure what it was, but we definitely had a special energy going on. In truth Justo spoke very little English and I spoke no Spanish, but we managed to communicate somehow. I got the vibe that Justo was very much into understanding the street, and for me, it was the same. You see, I was fascinated by the study of street orientated combat, and the functionality and practicality within the western world. I have a very inquisitive brain, always have had, I am never satisfied with a one dimensional answer to a problem, I will seek and search for as many variables as possible, knowing that in truth the answers are limited only by the capabilities of our minds.

So, I said to Justo at the end of the weekend trip that I'd get my Spanish friend back home to call him so I could set up a return trip to Spain. I did that, and that was to be the beginning of a great journey in the early days. I really liked where he was coming from as we truly did seem to be both reading from the same page, and that's ultimately why we clicked. In the early days we had a great relationship and really got on well, hence we both started travelling back and forth between England and Spain. During that time frame we worked on our personal flavour of training whilst at the same time we were still following our origins, that being the path of JKD, Kali, and Silat.

I really enjoyed the training that Justo and myself were developing, I enjoyed it a lot. I started struggling though teaching some of the classical "techniques" from the other arts as much of the training didn't feed what I was looking for. It just didn't give me what I wanted. I think all the arts are great, and I truly do, but something was missing, it just didn't give Andy Norman what Andy Norman was looking for. Due to these realities that I was feeling, I told Justo that I was struggling to teach certain things as I wasn't "feeling" the work, all due to my anarchic character. I'm an all or nothing kind of character, it has its good point and it's not so good points. I told Justo that I was more excited about what we were playing with behind the scenes. I wanted to do that. I said to Justo, why don't we start teaching what we love doing the most, Justo was a bit apprehensive about the suggestion, but after many long talks he eventually agreed and thought we should follow our dreams. So I made the push to follow our dreams, so it was in the year 2000 that KFM, Keysi fighting method got launched on to the main stream circuit. This was totally on the understanding that it could cost us everything which it pretty much did as I got disowned and sent to Coventry by pretty much everyone and that was for me having a dream. A lot of people said to me at the time, who the fuck do you think you are? I was shocked by the verbal attacks, but I simply replied, I'm Andy Norman and I have a dream! That's it. After only a few short years working on and pushing KFM we caught the attention of Hollywood, and in 2004 got called to audition for *Batman Begins!*

How did that come about?

At the time I was training Buster Reeves, an already internationally renowned stuntman, who also just happened to be the stunt double for Christian Bale on *Batman Begins.* I was in Germany teaching a seminar and I got a call from Buster, he asked if I would like to audition for a movie, but wouldn't tell me what it was, he said it was something called the `Intimidation Game` I thought it sounded like some weird Japanese TV program where people beat each other up with Jellyfish or what not. So I was a little reluctant at first, but said okay! Buster asked me to give him a call when I returned from Germany and we'd set it up. 2 weeks later I was back in the UK and driving back home from my academy one night with my wife; it was about 11pm in the evening. I suddenly got an urge to call Buster, it was a weird feeling, I just thought I need to ring Buster. It was one of these really strange moments in life, one where you just get a feeling! I HAD to ring Buster. So I rang up and just told him I was following up from our previous conversation. Buster said to me he'd see me in the morning at the studios, I was slightly taken back, as I had absolutely no idea what he was talking about! He said to me, "didn't Dave ring you; you have an audition in the morning"! I was like "OMG, no, I've heard nothing", Buster said: "well, you need to be here at Shepperton Film Studios in the morning". So I made a call to Paul Strauther, now Paul has been training with me all his life and is a great talent in his own right, I asked him if he could come down to the studio with me. He said sure, so we travelled down to the studio, and a long story short-ish, we entered the studios, did our meet and greet then walked into a massive rehearsal studio.

There are tons of people in it, running up walls, doing back flips and all sorts! Some seriously talented, fit, acrobatic kids! As people know, I'm not so much in to the acrobatic style, I'm a little more solid and just want the fighting aspect so I thought to myself, oh my god, I am so out of my depth here! What the fuck am I doing in here?! If this is what they're looking for, I'm not it, this isn't me at all! The crew came in and introduced themselves and started with auditions for all the ninjas in *Batman Begins.*

Again, that really wasn't my kind of thing, so I took a deep breath and said, listen guys, this isn't really what I do, would you allow me to show you what I do. There was this silence then some of the stunt guys and Paul Jennings just looked at me. I was thinking they thought who the fuck do you think you are?! Then the words "okay" rang out! So I stepped out onto the floor and did my thing. I was asked lots of questions and asked to show a variety of different things, which I did.

I showed some weapon training, a little bit of Kali. I was asked if I could show some jumping takedowns, so again I did, I showed a few bits from Silat. Then I showed them the `Thinking Man` from KFM, one of our signature "moves" back then. This quickly caught everybody's attention, and I was asked to show more. Paul Jennings came over after I'd finished showcasing some of my work, and said,

"I've been in this game a very long time, but Andy, you have something special going on. Paul Strauther and myself were asked to stay for lunch, and then after some of the stunt guys asked if we would stay and teach them some more stuff, of course we did! It just so happened that Christopher Nolan was looking for something a little more "raw" and not so theatrical …

On leaving the studio that day, I was told they were going to fire the video footage over to LA where it would be shown to Chris Nolan. I was also told that I would get a call within the next week letting me know if they wanted to employ me. A week later, Sunday morning, I'll never forget it… I got a call from the studio offices, I'd got the job as fight consultant on *Batman Begins,* and that's when it hit me, what the hell was going on! It was an awesome "oh my god" moment. I had just been employed by Warner Brothers as a fight consultant. From a phone call with Buster, to a freaky phone call I made, to auditions and eventually being employed by Warner Brothers. It was to be a moment that changed my life!

KFM by 2004 was already growing nicely, but touching Hollywood sent us global literally overnight. We became active in around 100+ countries and supported many of the followers with an online training university. When I got the job with Warner Brothers, Justo asked me when we were going to be starting, and I said, to be honest they only need one fight consultant. I had been invited and luckily they liked what they saw. But a few days later I did ring the production office and basically asked if they could employ my friend. Obviously the reaction was laughter! They simply said to me why we would employ two people when it's a one-man job. I then explained that we work as a unit and work as a partnership, eventually they said ok, they'd give it a go. I managed to convince the production office and the fight arranger to let me bring my mate to work! I don't know how I pulled that off, but I did! If I hadn't done that, I would not have managed to get Justo Dieguez into Hollywood.

Sadly many years down the line the KFM split; classic business split, we had completely different views on how to lead our lives and run the business, and ultimately where the journey was going. Justo's great, he has his way and his journey, but ultimately in the end it wasn't for me. Justo has continued with Keysi by Justo, and I've gone on to build the Defence Lab. For me Defence Lab simply reflects the way I approach things; a lab of investigation, I love to experiment with things, to see what works and if there are issues with functionality why, and can they be put right.

How do you think Defence Lab fits into the rest of the martial arts out there? Is the state of martial arts good at the moment?

At the time of the writing of this book, I think the martial arts world is in a strange place. There are a lot of good things going on, but also a lot of problems in the industry, so it's a very contradictory time. We live in a very westernised, monetised, concrete jungle. I think the philosophy of the arts can confuse people sometimes. In the western world, nothing is for free, and whether we like it or not, life is about money, life itself is a business. Why do people teach? They want to transmit their knowledge to others, but in order to do that you need a place to teach from. You usually need to pay for that privilege, hence it instantly becomes a business whether you like it or not. If you're training 4 people in your garage, who's paying your mortgage? You're paying money for them to train in the garage. It costs money to teach people regardless of who it is. If you have an academy, you need to pay the landlord or he'll kick you out. It would be great if people could simply stop bickering and arguing and just understand how the world works, and how money, sadly, runs all our lives. If you're not running a martial arts business for a full time income, then more often than not you'll work to subsidise your hobby. You can still be passionate about your art, as I am, and I have never watered down what I do in order to try and make a living from teaching. I'm simply an anarchic person, people love me, people hate me, and I'm fine with that, its life, but I've never gone down the road of selling out and going just to make a buck, it's not me. If you truly love what you do, and teach it with a passion, then people will feel it. BE YOURSELF.

If you have a dream, chase it; see if you can build a nice, successful and healthy organisation, an organisation that people enjoy belonging to. If you do that, then there's a very great chance you'll be able to make a great living from something you love to do, isn't that what we all want anyway?

I built KFM into a global entity, no matter what people think or say, it was a massive organisation that touched the world, but sadly it imploded due to Justo and myself parting ways. But not being one to be discouraged I set off to build yet another global branded organisation, which I've done. Defence Lab launched in 2012, within 2 years, 2014; the results could be clearly seen by simply watching the DL World Conference video on YouTube, and you can clearly see what we built from nothing. Global again.

Defence Lab is almost 4 years old now (2012 - 2016) and we have a huge global organisation with a very simple ethos behind it; we've created a healthy training environment that people simply enjoy being around. We try and give people the guidance and education on the realities of running a successful academy. We also educate on how to then expand an academy, and open multi locations. There is nothing wrong with running a great academy and making a good living, that is not called selling out or ripping people off, it's called intelligent. If you can make an environment that people love being in and around, you teach them great stuff and look after them, then they'll probably stay and train for a long time. In truth it's a very simple concept.

Sadly the word business and martial arts really struggles to mix. The idea is if you do well or earn money people hate you and think you're a sell out and a fraud. All because you're trying to get £50 from someone to teach what you've been sweating, bleeding and living for most of your life. A basketball player can run around on court and throw a ball into a basket and get 85 million dollars a year, and that is cool eh! Let's just put that in balance, they put a ball in a basket, that's their contribution to the world, for which they receive tens of millions of dollars, But if you're a martial artist and trying to get £45 a month from someone for their training which may have taken you 20/30 years to acquire the knowledge, then you're seen as a rip off merchant. It devalues everything. A solicitor can send you a letter and it'll cost you £500 and that's cool. You do your 20-30 year training and are a bad person if you charge £50 per month. The world is based on profit regardless of what you do.

If somebody is running a school with 1000 active people paying, then he must be doing something right. People who pay don't stay if they're not happy, it's that simple. Not everybody is looking for the toughest bad ass martial art out there. Many people are simply happy doing what they like doing. People aren't forced to stay at academies, they choose to be there. Don't get me wrong, there are lots of not so great teachers out there, and I'm sure the McDojo name emerged for a reason, BUT, not all schools that are doing really well are McDojo's.

If you're looking for the art of taekwondo, because you like it, then that's awesome. It's not for me personally, I can't do all those amazing jumping spinning kicks, if I tried, well, I would definitely be going to hospital, but I respect it if taught well.

Talk to us about the tri-branding then?

For me personally, I'm always inspired by many things in life. I have a brain that operates out of the box. Several years ago I observed how many of the major corporations were merging, I watched as the music industry followed with super stars such as Christina Aguilera began singing with some of the world's greatest rappers. Previously that would have been thought to be pretty un-cool, but suddenly rappers started buying Christina Aguilera CDs and vice versa. You cross-brand and you network and make friends. Every martial artist is trying to show their art to the world. A healthy way to do that is to have friends and network.

Another sad aspect of the martial arts is the idea that, for example, I study street, and someone else studies Judo, therefore I can't be friends with them or speak to them. Of course I can! I can be their friend and cross brand. I started my journey with Bob and we've gone full circle, and I met Phil Norman very early on that journey too. We've all found our own specific journeys. Bob was the Godfather of JKD and Kali in Europe and pioneered the cultural movement there. Phil puts his flavour on everything via the Ghost Elusive Combat System, and now 20-30 years later DL has a nice twist on street fighting. Are Defence Lab, Ghost or 4D combat the best arts out there? Who knows eh... how do you really answer that one? We can't! But are they cool and funky? We think so. We don't think we're better than everyone else, we just like putting a new twist on things, that's all. The tri-branding offers up 3 individuals who have had a bit of a journey! Love us or hate us, we've followed our paths and 20-30 years later we've our expressions of what we feel…

The future of Defence Lab for me in a nutshell. I'd like to complete my dream of being healthy, looking after my family, and make it through the rest of my life! I'd like to finish the dream that I set off with as a young lad.

I want to continue to transmit and express what I like and feel, whilst building a global network, a network that will also allow others to find their own dreams too. DL is creating a great martial art learning environment, one that will then enable people to go home and potentially build their own dreams of becoming a teacher or school owner. I don't want anything more. Just something that's nice and works and without sounding too cheesy, tries to help people. live the dream and share the dream. People need drivers, but I don't necessarily want people to follow me. People follow others if you treat them well and share a common goal. If you're nice to people, they'll be nice back. I just want to build a nice place to be that can function and build people's lives. Hopefully the organisation can help people to find their own dreams in the martial arts and then build them.

Conclusion

So there we have it! 15 interviews with 15 of the best martial artists in the UK. It was fascinating to hear about their lives, their inspirations and what they hope to achieve in the martial arts, but one thing really stood out from all the interviews for me. Every martial artist featured in this volume was passionate about the art they teach and teach for other people, to improve other people and build them up. These martial artists are dedicated with a wealth of experience in real world scenarios, and also in teaching and training, yet they all talk about their students and doing the best for them.

These individuals are at the peak of their skill level and have followings all around the world and it just goes to show that if you put in the effort and keep training, we can all achieve something very special within the martial arts. Everyone featured in the book was happy to be featured alongside one another and there was no `bitching` about others – this is exactly why they were chosen for the book. The martial arts are unique in the fact that they seem so charged by politics and style v style bickering. Those involved with these books openly train with others, learn from others and in the case of Andy, Bob and Phil even work with each other to further develop a brand. This revolutionary kind of thinking is what sets them apart. Most people interviewed in this edition agreed that the martial arts were in a strange place and that there were some keeping traditions and standards alive, and others bickering and selling out. Let's hope that the fantastic individuals in this book are the ones flying the flag for the UK and abroad and are the ones taking martial arts to another level and increasing its exposure for future generations.

Myself and Lucci hope you've enjoyed this edition of *Martial Masters Vol. 1* and would like to extend our deepest gratitude to those who have helped in one way or another with the book. From family members proof reading first drafts, to the fantastic individuals featured in this book we thank you all for helping us to produce this book which aims to bring the best martial artists together regardless of style and system.

This is just the start for myself and Lucci so look out soon for Volumes 2, 3, 4 and even an international edition maybe!

About the authors:

Dan Holloway

Dan has been involved in martial arts for nearly 20 years and currently runs Defence Lab Lincoln. He also holds a 3rd Degree black belt in Yoshinkan Aikido and has trained in many other arts including jiu-jitsu, MMA, karate and KFM. He runs his own successful blog `The Martial View` and is passionate about promoting martial arts for the many benefits they can bring. The main man behind the writing of this book, Dan has enjoyed speaking with so many top instructors and martial artists, finding out more about their lives and developing the project so that it's ready for you guys to read! A *Martial Arts Illustrated* Hall of Famer Dan is committed to promoting quality martial arts and quality martial artists which is his hope for this book.

Lucci Del-Gaudio

Luciano (Lucci) Del-Gaudio started his Martial Arts journey back in the 80s . After watching Bruce Lee's *Enter the Dragon* as a 9-year-old boy he started Karate in his home town of Sneinton, Nottingham. Lucci, who comes from a Martial Arts family, has 5 older Brothers all at Dan Grade in Ju-Jitsu. 1 of Lucci's brothers, Frank, took Lucci under his wing and became his Ju-Jitsu teacher for many years. During his Ju-Jitsu training Lucci started to explore the world of martial arts. He took up amateur Boxing and Thai Boxing. During the '90s, Lucci discovered Geoff Thomson and started to get involved with Reality Based martial arts. He started to find interest in fighting arts such as Krav Maga. Lucci has always put his Ju-Jitsu as his first love followed by Reality Based Self Defence. Today, Lucci teachers Combat Ju-Jitsu, a format of Ju-Jitsu and Reality-based Self Defence in his own Academy in Nottingham.